The
Power of
Coaching

The Secrets of Achievement

by
Machen MacDonald

With Co-Authors:

- Harry Hoopis
- Robert Chiron
- Brian Tracy
- Chet Holmes
- Robert Irwin
- Yasmine Bijan
- Debra Satterwhite
- Scott Taylor
- Brett Bauer
- Don Boyer
- Rich Campe
- Jim Rohn
- Diane Ruebling
- Denis Waitley
- Ed Deutschlander
- Germaine Porché
- Jed Niederer

The Power of Coaching
The Secrets of Achievement
Published by PLI Publishing
www.ThePowerOfCoaching.com
530-273-8000
Grass Valley, California

Copyright © 2007 ProBrilliance Leadership Institute (PLI)
Library of Congress Control Number: 2007931395
ISBN: 978-1-4243-4422-2

Cover Design by Taylor Made Marketing
scott@fastpathcoaching.com

Editing, Composition, and Typography by Michelle McKenzie
michellemckenzie@hughes.net

This book is available at quantity discounts for bulk purchase.
For more information, contact:
www.ThePowerOfCoaching.com
Telephone: 530-273-8000
Grass Valley, California

Special Note: This edition of "The Power of Coaching – The Secrets of Achievement" is designed to provide information and motivation to our readers. It is sold with the understanding, that the publisher is not engaged to render any type of psychological, legal, or any other kind of professional advice. The content of each article is the sole expression and opinion of its author, and not that necessarily of the publisher. No warranties or guarantees are expressed or implied by the publisher's choice to include any of the content in this volume. Neither the publisher nor the individual author(s) shall be liable for any physical, psychological, emotional, financial, or commercial damages, including but not limited to special, incidental, consequential or other damages. Our view and rights are the same: You are responsible for your own choices, actions, and results.

Printed in the United States of America

Praise for
The Power of Coaching...
The Secrets of Achievement!

"I have been training and coaching coaches for more than 25 years.

Many of the newer coaches who have entered the field recently only want to sell you something. Some of these newer coaches seem more interested in their own economic well-being than in yours.

The coaches in **The Power of Coaching** are completely different. These coaching superstars collectively possess several hundred years of coaching wisdom.

Perhaps most importantly, they genuinely want to help you achieve and live the life of your dreams.

Moreover, these coaches have the tools and expertise to help you do so. These are truly some of the "best of the best" coaches in the world today.

Your minimal investment in purchasing a copy of **The Power of Coaching** should be returned to you 1,000 times over or more if you follow the wisdom contained in this remarkable book.

Several dozen authors each year ask me to endorse their books on coaching, personal growth, success strategies and investing. I have recommended very few books over the years. As much as my busy coaching and consulting schedule permit, I read them all. Very few make the grade. **The Power of**

Coaching is an exception. This is one of the few books I can wholeheartedly endorse. <u>This book could change your life</u>. "

—**Donald Moine, Ph.D.**
Coach to Professional Coaches
"Learn from the best of the best."
www.DrMoine.com

"If you are looking to raise your coaching game, you must read this book." —**John Assaraf**
Author, Speaker, Entrepreneur, Founder
OneCoach, Inc.
www.OneCoach.com

"Learn from proven field leaders and professional coaches what it really takes to coach people to the next level."
—**"Coach Conk" Buckley**
GAMA Past President and
Essentials of Leadership Facilitator

"The Power of Coaching is full of practical ways to develop the crucial and important skill of coaching."
—**Lou Cassara**, CEO & Founder,
The Cassara Clinic, LLC
www.cassaraclinic.com

"The ideas and strategies in this book will inspire you to take action...the right action that gets dramatic results."
—**Eva Gregory**, Master Coach, Speaker and
Author of *The Feel Good Guide to Prosperity*
www.leadingedgecoaching.com

"The Power of Coaching shows you how to understand your team and bring out their best." —**Jan Rosen**
Agency Sales Director MetLife

"If you are a part of a team or lead one, this book will be one of your most valuable tools. It's packed with practical and tactical coaching tools and processes to assist you and your team to be completely aligned with the outcomes you desire. This is truly good stuff!"

—**Jeanna Gabellini**
MasterPeace Coaching & Training
Co-author of Life Lessons:
Mastering the Law of Attraction
www.masterpeacecoaching.com

"At some time in our business life, we all can get off center no matter how successful we have been. Machen's book is a tremendous resource to remind, refocus, and reengage the important coaching we do."

—**Jim Fischer**
Managing Partner Thrivent Financial

"There is no need to re-invent the coaching wheel. This book is full of insights, experiences, and advice on how to build a successful coaching practice. Read the advice… then put it into practice!

—**Jim Horan** – Author, Speaker,
Consultant, President,
The One Page Business Plan Co.
www.onepagebusinessplan.com

"The Power of Coaching is a 'must have' tool for your coaching toolbox, and one you'll leverage over and over to help create the powerful results your clients want and need."

- **Todd Mauney**, President & Master Coach
Rich Campe International

"The Power of Coaching offers unique and refreshing guidance to help us each develop our coaching skills. I scribbled notes on almost every page. I will refer to this book over and over again."

—James G. Kerchner – President Diversified Solutions
Consultant Self Management Group
www.diversified-solutions.com
www.self-managment.com

"Read The Power of Coaching and discover how to once and for all coach the people you lead and get measurable results."

—Jeffrey Plummer, CLU – Associate Managing Partner,
John Hancock Financial Network

Acknowledgements

To my family for living the inspired life! You make it all worthwhile and fun!

To **Michelle McKenzie** for taking our thoughts and words and assembling them in such a way to perpetuate the wisdom and contribution of our authors.

To **Scott Taylor** for your professionalism, creativity, dedication and friendship. You have so much to offer the world on so many levels. I am thankful that I have been blessed to experience your work.

To **Jed Niederer** and **Germaine Porche'** for bringing great levity to our book through your wonderful cartoons.

To **Brett Bauer** for opening up your world to inspire others so that they can accomplish more.

To **Rich Campe** for leading the way in thinking huge and acting huge and bringing about huge results. It all starts with the thinking!

To **Todd Mauney** for your generous contribution and focus in supporting the coaching community.

To **Diane Ruebling** for your friendship and focus on the power of peer to peer accountability. We tend to step up to the level at which others see us. Thanks for seeing me at higher and higher levels.

To **Harry Hoopis** for expecting so much of so many and having such a powerful vision of what's possible for them. You are a true inspiration. Thanks for choosing to be the hero long ago.

To **Dr. Bob Chiron** for your professional and provocative dialogue during the recent year. You have sparked many great ideas that have come to pass.

To **Ed Deutschlander** for your leadership by example and allowing so many to witness what is possible when you are true to yourself and committed to excellence.

To **Dr. Rob Irwin** for conveying neuroscience in a way that so many people can take control of their lives and careers.

To **Dr. Denis Waitley** for sharing your wisdom of doing within while doing without. It all starts on the inside.

To **Yasmine Bijan** for your energy, charm and setting the tone for this book.

To **Deb Satterwhite** thanks for illuminating the way on such an important path. Your perspective and insights are a blessing. I cherish our friendship.

To **Brian Tracy** for your ongoing creation and refinement of promotional acumen.

To **Chet Holmes** for sharing such superior and proven models leading to rapid and dramatic results.

To **Ralph Napolitano** for your help in pulling together important contributions to the book.

To **Don Boyer**, what can I say...it is a blast playing with you on the increasing levels of reality. I am so proud of you and beyond excited regarding The Mentor Movie. I am proud and humbled to be a part of your ongoing projects.

To **Jim Rohn** for ridiculing the ridiculous and putting servant leadership in such an inviting and intoxicating light.

To **Mickey Straub** for your friendship, alliance and dedication. Your heartfelt foreword is a gift I will always cherish.

To **God** for all that is, was and ever will be.

> **"Genius is the ability to reduce the complicated to the simple."**
>
> **– C.W. Ceran**

TABLE OF CONTENTS

Introduction		14
Chapter 1	Yasmine Bijan	18
	Coaching: What's So Great About That?	
Chapter 2	Harry Hoopis & Robert Chiron	34
	Capturing True Desires: A New Coaching Paradigm	
Chapter 3	Ed Deutschlander	44
	Be Faithful to What is Helpful	
Chapter 4	Machen MacDonald	56
	Business Plans Made Easy	
Chapter 5	Denis Waitley	64
	From Motivation to Motive-Action	
Chapter 6	Brett Bauer & Rich Campe	70
	Is Your Ladder Leaning Against the Right Wall?	
Chapter 7	Diane Ruebling	88
	Emotional Competence: The Path to Achievement	
Chapter 8	Chet Holmes	96
	The Ultimate Method for Developing Master Level Salespeople	
Chapter 9	Robert Irwin	102
	New Pathways for Success	
Chapter 10	Brian Tracy	112
	Think Like a Winner	
Chapter 11	Scott Taylor	118
	Imagine Create Deliver: A Foundation of Achievement	
Chapter 12	Don Boyer	128
	The Hidden Secret of Achievement	
Chapter 13	Jim Rohn	134
	Preparations for Your Presentations	
Chapter 14	Debra Satterwhite	142
	Define it! Build it! Own it!	
Chapter 15	Machen MacDonald	153
	What if Socrates was Your Coach?	
Cartoons	Germaine Porché and Jed Niederer	158

Foreword

Several years ago, I walked into a training room to meet someone I had only spoken with by telephone previously. Fortunately for me, he was in from California and happened to be visiting an office in the Chicago suburbs just a few blocks away.

I don't remember being particularly stressed that day, but as I walked into the training room, he looked up from his computer, stood up and shook hands and I felt a sense of calmness. It was as if time stopped, or at least slowed down for a moment. His name? Machen MacDonald.

You are in for a treat. Machen's brilliance shines in two rare abilities...his ability to calm a room when he enters and to bring people together for a common cause. These are two signs of a great leader. The people that Machen has assembled for "The Power of Coaching" are here to help you lead, and are some of the most impacting leaders in their chosen fields. Many I know personally, others only through their writing. They have learned from the masters and have become masters themselves.

Have you ever wondered why one business succeeds and another one fails? Have you ever noticed one agency, airline, car dealership or department store flourish while another one flounders? There could be many extenuating factors, but none greater than leadership. Great products can camouflage bad leadership for a while, but nothing takes the place of good leadership. Your role is omnipotent. The lives and welfare of many are in your hands.

So, what can you expect to get from reading this book? In a word, "Optimize". You'll get to optimize your time (something that is near and dear to my heart) and leverage yourself. You also have the opportunity to optimize talents, for reading "The Power of Coaching" can have a profound impact on your talents and those of others if you choose to take action on some of the principles herein.

It has been said that you'll be the same person twelve months from now except for the people that you meet and the books that you read. This is one of the greatest advantages of this book. You get to accomplish both.

Live, Love, Inspire and Serve,

Mickey Straub, President
Sales Activity Management, Inc.

Introduction

"Our chief want in life is someone who will make us do what we can."
- Emerson

You have this book in your hands because you are a leader. You have developed the sacred skills of attracting ideal people into your organization and regularly enlightening them on how to quench their thirst for becoming more of who they can be. You have successfully crossed the rivers and chasms they are now approaching. Your passion is to help them navigate successfully. You have ascended the mountain to see the new vistas of what is possible and you have come down off those peaks and into the valley so you could ascend again and this time to an even higher peak. These great experiences allow and empower you to show others how to live a greater life by design. From these experiences, you possess an abundance of wisdom to offer the people you lead. Avoid discounting your experience and achievement, for it is the fiber of your leadership.

I believe all people have a unique innate talent, genius or gift. I call this your brilliance. It is my passion and purpose to provoke brilliance in as many people as I possibly can. By provoking I mean to literally "call forth" the brilliance within people so they can experience living a fuller life.

I do this one on one, with small groups and with audiences of hundreds, even thousands. I am fortunate enough to perpetuate these key messages via books, audio and video as well. It is basically leveraging the ripple effect. By you reading this book and having your brilliance provoked, you are allowing the dissemination of that awareness one fold, ten fold, perhaps 100 fold or more. It's this ability for magnification that increases one's value.

"People who are coaches will be the norm. Other people won't get promoted." —Jack Welch, when CEO, of General Electric

---

Coaching, in its truest form, is not telling people how to do something or to do it better, but rather it is facilitating others to see the most empowering perspective of how to expedite their success and fulfillment in relation to their circumstances.

I'm sure you have read a plethora of books on leadership and management. You have attended the workshops and have the hats, mugs and binders to prove it. That is necessary and good.

However, the lines of coaching, leadership and management are often blurred. It is the intent of the selected authors of this book to provide you the perspective of what coaching is and how to be a stronger coach. We will do this by enhancing your awareness, knowledge and skill of your coaching talent and capacity in the realm of management and leadership.

"I absolutely believe that people, unless coached, never reach their maximum potential." - Bob Nardelli, when CEO of Home Depot

---

It is said that a manager gets in your face and a coach gets in your head. A majority of the coaching-benefit does not necessarily occur during the actual session you have with the people you lead. It's what happens in between those sessions—the real life-events—that integrate the learning from session to session. Coaching is helping the people you are working with to align their awareness, action and accountability. Coaching is propelling them authentically into who they really are and helping them to accomplish what they really want to accomplish. In essence, coaching, and this book, will show you how to influence people to live the abundant lives they are destined to live.

In these pages, you will hear from world class business coaches who are leaders in the coaching community in every sense of the word. You will also hear from top producers and managers who have reached the zenith of their profession through their outstanding coaching ability and coaching experiences.

As with the other books in this series you need not read from cover to cover to benefit, although we are certain you will want to. You may simply wish to peruse the index and start with the chapter title that most grabs your attention. Trust that the one you start with is the right one for you.

Because of the overwhelming response to our first collaborative anthology, The Power of Coaching; Engaging Excellence In Others, we continue our dedication in providing coaching strategies, models and stories for the leader looking to enhance their acumen as it relates to helping the people they lead realize their potential.

Congratulations on affecting others so profoundly and thank you for allowing us to share our inside insights that may help in that endeavor. Here's to Provoking Your Brilliance and to you provoking the brilliance in others!

Machen MacDonald

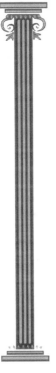

Yasmine Bijan is a highly sought after world class speaker, Certified Professional Coach, and published author. She is featured as a *Master Mentor* in a film to be released December, 2007 called, *"The Power of Mentorship, The Movie - Unlock the Journey to Success."* Yasmine founded *InPowerU Success Coaching,* a coaching, training, and consulting firm. Having worked in Corporate America for 13 years, Yasmine coaches her clients to create success by focusing on their passion and strengths in conjunction with applied business practices commonly used by Fortune 500 companies. Her services include keynote speaking, individual and group coaching, workshops, and tele-classes.

You can contact Yasmine at Yasmine@inpoweru.com, or 858-922-5350. You may also visit www.inpoweru.com or www.AskYasmine.com.

Chapter 1

Coaching:
What's so Great About That?

Yasmine Bijan

I know that you might have some skepticism about the *Power of Coaching.* You may even feel a sense of overwhelm when reading this book, and doubt that coaching could create exponential growth for you and your team. However, the fact that you chose to read this book means that you are motivated to take yourself and your team to the next level. In this book, you'll realize how these simple, proven techniques will be invaluable to your team's performance, job satisfaction, productivity, and overall life.

In this chapter, you will learn fundamental coaching techniques to inspire excellence in yourself and your team.

You will learn:
- Simple questions to ask that will 'explode' with results when coaching your team
  - Innovative ways to engage yourself and your team in coaching
  - What to look and listen for when you are coaching a team member
  - How to benchmark off of Professional Coaching practices in your one-on-one meetings
  - Let's begin with asking simple questions. Questions are the springboard to engaging, discovering, and

empowering yourself and your team. How you and your team answer these questions will provide a certain perspective or awareness so pay close attention to the answers the come up.

Let's use the topic of coaching as an example in asking engaging questions.

Engaging Sample Questions:
- When you think of coaching, what comes to mind?
- What do you see the role of a coach is?
- What have you heard about coaching?
- How would you describe the impact of someone who has been a "coach" for you?
- Why would coaching be beneficial in your career?
- Where would coaching support you or your team in achieving better results?
- What could a Professional Coach do for you and your team?

Possible Answers:
- Focus
- Action
- Commitment
- Teamwork
- Implementation
- Motivation
- Feedback
- Support
- Encouragement
- Inspiration
- Development
- Achievement
- Guidance
- Mentorship
- Leadership
- Consistency

Such simple, yet powerful, questions are asked frequently in coaching. Asking the right questions will reveal a clear perspective. Once a clear perspective has been identified, you and your team will begin to see, hear, or notice new possibilities, experiences, outcomes, ideas, and solutions. Asking the right questions will also reveal any obstacles that could impede progress.

Think of yourself as a detective looking for clues. Here are different ways you can detect them. For instance, how you and your team perceive issues, topics, solutions, and ideas offers tremendous clues. The clues are in the answers that come up to the questions being asked. The clues become more obvious when you regularly identify the "thinking processes and patterns" (such as the beliefs, attitudes, and perceptions). It becomes even clearer as you pay attention to what you and your team are saying that impact behaviors and actions.

For example, as you read the above questions, did you notice how you responded? Would you have responded differently if you read the answers first? How did it engage you in exploring your thoughts, emotions, reactions, actions, or outcomes? What opinions did you notice you had about coaching?

Likely, you responded based on your own past experiences, knowledge, and perception about coaching or coaches. Many people associate coaching with athletic coaching. Perhaps you revisited memories of your coach or team leader of an activity you participated in when you were young, such as Little League, Pop Warner Football, soccer, tennis, gymnastics, or on a swim team. Maybe you watched sports on television where coaches were present. You probably had opinions about the coach of your favorite sports team. Maybe you reflected on a different kind of coach you worked with. You may even have had thoughts or comparisons about your own effectiveness in coaching your team members.

Again, how you and your team respond to questions will provide insights into the way you and your team think and act. Thereby, creating either the results you want or results you don't want.

Here's the thing. If you and your team think coaching works, you're right. If you and your team think coaching doesn't work, you're right. Either way, you're right! No matter how you answered the above questions, you were right. Why? Because it is YOUR perception! Therefore, in your perception, you are right. However, your perception versus someone else's perception may differ. Therein lays the challenge that causes miscommunication and ineffectiveness in the workplace. Powerful questions are a way to access perceptions that are invaluable to discover.

Using the coaching theme as an example, your team members may or may not embrace coaching as a practice. In turn, that will either have you and your team catapult results, or hinder results you want to achieve. If coaching is a necessary skill to elicit excellence from you and your team, it doesn't work to have a belief that coaching is ineffective, right? Therefore, a shift in clarity, awareness, and understanding of your own and your team's perspectives are critical factors in taking your team to the next level.

Imagine asking similar questions in the example above, but instead of it being about coaching, it's about you and your team. Consider questions that are about you or your team members' careers, performance, goals, results, ideas, vision, dreams, passions, strengths, and blocks. What would that open up?

Engaging your team by asking simple and powerful questions allows for new perspectives, solutions, and actions to show up.

This coaching technique also provides opportunities to grow. Sometimes it's uncomfortable to grow. Therefore, challenge yourself to be "coachable" and uncomfortable. Keep in mind, that to be an effective coach it is best to be "coachable" yourself. So, as you read this chapter, identify how you can apply these concepts to yourself first. Then, learn how you can apply them to your team. Once you see, hear, discover, or understand how you operate, you are far more effective in providing coaching support for other people.

The following is another innovative way to engage you and your team in a simple coaching process that uncovers different perspectives. This is a tool to assist you in peeling away the layers of a particular topic or issue. The technique is to ask the question, *"What's so great about that?"* after each response.

Asking "What's So Great About That?" as a technique to explore the topic of perspective:

Discovering and understanding perspective is important.

What is so great about that?

It will lead to more clarity about your point of view or the point of view of the person being coached.

What's so great about that?

When you have more clarity about your point of view, or of the person being coached, you can be more effective in addressing issues, topics, beliefs, reactions, actions, and results or outcomes.

What's so great about that?

23

When you are more effective at addressing particular matters, it allows for more opportunities to make better choices.

What's so great about that?

When you have more opportunities and make better choices, you produce better results.

What's so great about that?

When you produce better results, you experience more recognition, communication, job satisfaction, leadership, and accomplishments.

What's so great about that?

Satisfied employees are more loyal, attrition goes down, and productivity goes up.

What's so great about that?

When attrition goes down and productivity and results goes up, everyone is happy!!!!

What's so great about that?

When everyone is happy, it's a much more empowering and fulfilling environment to work within.

The simple question, *"What's so great about that?"* is extremely effective. Powerful, insightful questions are the backbone to the *Power of Coaching*. When you answer powerful questions that only you know the answer to, new perspectives are revealed. The people being coached are the ones who know the most about their own vast experiences, knowledge, skills, strengths, weaknesses, education, background, beliefs, culture, upbringing, perceptions, and *THINKING*. Using powerful questions is one of the main principles that distinguish coaching from consulting, mentoring, or training.

Next, look and listen for clues such as lack-of-commitment to achieving goals, incongruence, confusion, or gossip. Compare these to seeing, hearing, or sensing a positive attitude towards commitment, alignment, clarity, and teamwork. By inquiring into the *THINKING* (thoughts, beliefs, attitudes, or perceptions), you can predict or reveal clues that can impact change.

The following simple diagram will assist you in discovering clues which will not only provide more clarity for yourself, but for the people you coach or lead.

Thinking/Beliefs/Perceptions →
   Responses/Reactions/Emotions →
      Actions/Commitment →
         Results/Outcomes/Goals

Therefore, if you want to shift results, first shift the thinking. The *THINKING* is at the core of any result, outcome, or goal. Ask insightful questions, then look and listen to what the answers reveal. Keep in mind, the questions aren't an interrogation process, rather, they are designed to be an inquiry. The inquiry unveils the *THINKING* and *BELIEFS* that will lead to how you and your team *FEELS, RESPONDS* or *REACTS*, which leads to the *ACTIONS* or *COMMITMENTS* taken, which leads to *RESULTS* and *OUTCOMES*.

What is so great about that?

You can transform, achieve results, and take action much more quickly and effectively when you look for your own answers versus being told the answers. However, when you investigate your own answers, the caveat is that it's human nature to want to be right about those answers. The irony is that there are no universally right answers. Therefore, the right answer for you may be different than someone else's right answer. Engaging in this exploration, you will see, hear, experience, or discover ways of thinking or being that will either serve you or not serve you or your team. The answers and discoveries will either move you and your team forward, or may keep you stuck. Often times, when you see answers for yourself, there is much greater openness to taking action, versus someone else giving the answers to you.

Think about a time when you came up with your own answer. How did you **RESPOND**? How might you have responded if your mom, dad, teacher, manager, or boss told you that same answer? Both were effective, yet had different outcomes. What was your reaction? What was the action you took? What was the outcome?

In the example of coaching as the topic, you and your team members will **RESPOND** positively or negatively to the process. Likely, if there is a negative response, there will be a lot of resistance to implementation. In turn, there likely will be little commitment. The lack of commitment will result in ineffectiveness. However, if a you and your team **RESPOND** positively to coaching, it's likely there will be openness to move forward and to take **ACTIONS** towards the desired outcome, goal, or result. This leads to better performance, job satisfaction, and productivity.

26

For example, let's say that you would like your team to follow up with clients more effectively, or to have your team submit their reports on time. They might **RESPOND** by not complying, perhaps because they lack commitment and accountability. Exploring their thoughts or perceptions about this matter is critical to causing a shift. You can then get to the source of what might *really* be going on. Perhaps their perception is that, "It's a waste of time." A positive **SHIFT** in that line of thinking would have them **RESPONDING** with an open mind. With an open mind now available, they would likely seek ways to take appropriate **ACTION**. In so doing, when they recognize it for themselves, they will likely take the steps to follow up with their clients or customers, or submit their reports on time, or reduce the distractions. That is the *Power of Coaching*.

Coaching goes hand in hand with training, mentorship, and consulting. So, if you are already doing so in your meetings, fantastic!

To demonstrate further the impact that coaching has on productivity, read the following case study, which showed the effectiveness of training alone, versus training plus coaching. The results were astounding.

Study performed by: Public Personal Management
Winter 1997
Volume 26 Issue 4 Page 461-469

"Compared training alone to coaching and training and found that training alone increased productivity by 24.7% and training plus coaching increased productivity by 88%.

Authors: Gerald Olivero, K. Denise Bane, Richard E. Kopelman

Classification Codes:
  9190 US
  9130: Experimental/Theoretical Treatment
  6200: Training and Development
  9550: Public Sector Organizations

Abstract: *A study examined the effects that executive coaching had on a public sector municipal agency. Thirty-one managers underwent a conventional managerial training program, which was followed by eight weeks of one-on-one executive coaching. Training increased the productivity by 24.7%. The coaching—which included goal setting, collaborative problem solving, practice, feedback, supervisory involvement, evaluation of end-results, and public presentation—increased productivity by 88.5%, a significantly greater gain compared to training alone. Descriptions of procedures, explanations for the desired results and suggestions for further results and practices were offered."*

With statistics like that, coaching is becoming more and more prevalent throughout the workforce.

Here is a final piece I would like to share with you. As a Professional Coach, I structure my sessions to include powerful questions to move my clients forward with velocity. You can benchmark off of them and incorporate them into your one-on-one meetings as coaching opportunities with your team members.

Sample Professional Coaching Session:

- What's been happening since we last spoke?
- What wins or challenges have occurred since then?
- What would you like to focus on today?
- Is there something specific you would like coaching on?

- What's missing? What's next?
- What are you going to take away from our coaching meeting today?
- What actions are you _committed_ to taking this week/month?
- Is there anything else you might like to say?
- What would you like to be recognized for?

These questions foster growth, trust, relationship, and opportunity for taking action.

Utilizing the *Power of Coaching* will support you and your team in closing that gap of where you are now to where you want to be. Clearly focus on where you and your team want to be! Much like athletic coaches have their teams focus on winning a game, you and your team can focus on winning yours. The key is to ACT AS IF you have already won. In doing so, the results you want will be achieved more quickly. Athletes use this process all the time. You can bring this to your meetings as well.

One thing to keep in mind, however, is that your team members and direct reports will have a different coaching dynamic with you than they would with a Professional Coach. The dynamics and the level of coaching will be different when working with Professional Coaches. Depending on your position, you may have the ability to promote or fire your team members. You may be accountable for the specific results they produce. Therefore, be aware that there is the possibility that your job responsibilities or position may not allow the same objectivity as that of a Professional Coach.

Highly trained Professional Coaches engage in these powerful techniques. Exploring different perspectives and ways of thinking are critical in evoking excellence from you and your team. New ways of **THINKING** and **BEING** will produce desired results more quickly.

Keep in mind that learning from a book is also quite different than actually experiencing and practicing the **Power of Coaching** directly. Seek ways to be open and "coachable" in taking your own life and career to new levels. As they say, the best students are the most effective teachers. The same goes with coaching! The most effective coaches are the most "coachable".

In this chapter, you have learned how to ask simple questions that can explode results in coaching your team. You have a deeper understanding of how to engage yourself and your team in the coaching process. You have discovered what to look and listen for when you are coaching a team member. You have an example of how to structure coaching techniques into your one-on-one meetings. Practice these principles and watch how they impact you and your team.

Thank you for investing your valuable time in reading this book. Clearly, you are committed to discovering more effective ways to create exponential growth for you and your team. My intention in writing this chapter is to have you see, hear, and experience how simple techniques are proven to be invaluable to your team's performance, communication, job satisfaction, and productivity. Enjoy the learning, stretching, and growing process in all of your endeavors.

"Motivation is what
gets you started.
Habit is what
keeps you going."

– Jim Ryun

**Although the Coach
will ordinarily err on
the side of asking
questions versus
giving advice,
sometimes
advice is appropriate.**

COACHING SOUP FOR THE CARTOON SOUL

Harry Hoopis, CLU, ChFC, is the Managing Partner of the *Hoopis Financial Group* of Northwestern Mutual in Chicago, IL, and CEO of the *Hoopis Performance Network*. He was inducted into the GAMA International Management Hall of Fame and is the principle author of *The Essentials of Management Development*. You can reach Harry Hoopis at 847-272-3130 or visit him on the web at www.hoopis.com

Robert Chiron, Ph.D. is a high impact organizational consultant with over 20 years experience in guiding businesses and individuals in the successful completion of organizational alignment and development through the use of his <u>Business Effectiveness Model</u> ™, bringing their now attainable goals to fruition.

Bob has shaped, directed and contributed to the Recruiting, Selection and Retention programs for Northwestern Mutual and it's Network Offices which also uses <u>The Evaluation Interview</u> which he is the co-author of and is currently in its 5th edition published by McGraw Hill. He has worked with over 20 Network Offices in the creation and execution of "alignment" expanding their capabilities and organizational structures. Bob has also been a Principle at the Hoopis Performance Network since its inception. You can contact Robert Chiron, rjc3340@aol.com

Chapter 2

Capturing "True Desires"
A New Coaching Paradigm to Achieve
Sustainable Results

Harry Hoopis and Robert Chiron

The old coaching paradigm no longer works. To test this hypothesis talk to people who were recently coached or who had recent coaching meetings. Ask them if they followed through on what was discussed from these coaching meetings. Next, ask them if they intend to act on all that was discussed. Typically, the answers range from somewhat to not at all. The two reasons for this lie in the fact that people today, must have buy-in/ownership to what is being worked on, which is called "alignment", and it has to be tied to their "true desires."

"Alignment": creating buy-in and ownership

Today's society is far different from the previous one. In former years people were told what to do and they simply did it out of some kind of loyalty or the belief that they "should" do it. Today, individuals need to identify with the "why" behind the what. This is called "alignment." This is different from what was used in the past to coach people. When people were told to do something they simply said, "yes" without thinking about the consequences of their decision. In other words, they complied with a request. As a result, there was very little follow-through and frustrations ensued from not seeing consistent coaching results.

This new mindset, moving from compliance to alignment, is critical in the coaching process. People need to have ownership in the things they do, explain why they need to do it, and believe that it can be done. Compliance conjures up feelings of constricted and, generally, negative rigid guidelines, and of being forced to do something. Alignment, on the other hand, brings up feelings of being on the same page, mutual agreement, buy-in and ownership. In this manner, coaching is a mutual process between the person being coached and his/her coach. The only measure in coaching is seeing someone take action. If nothing changes, then what really has been achieved?

This mindset is the centerpiece of the new coaching paradigm. Without developing "alignment", there can be little to no sustainable results. However, while pursing this lofty ideal, exciting results can be achieved and mutual expectations can be realized.

Capturing "true" desires: the new paradigm

Capturing "true" desires focuses on identifying those things that people want which they will take action on. The key to this process that produces a paradigm shift is helping people to "execute/act" on what is most important to them.

We all have goals, desires and dreams that we strive towards. However, these are so many in number that we will not consistently move forward on them. This is exactly what happens in a coaching relationship. We identify so many things to work on that we do not follow through. Psychologically, when we are confronted with too many tasks/goals, we end up feeling overwhelmed, we lose focus and we lose confidence. What happens to us at that point? Nothing!!! We tend to stop dead in our tracks. We know what we need to do, but we never get started. We look at the list of things to do and since it appears to be so daunting we put the list away for another day.

So, here is the process to capture "true" desires:

1. First, define what you want to change, what you need to do, or, simply what you want. Like most people your list will be quite long. This is a start. It allows you to think about what has been on your mind and/or what you want to change.

2. Second, take this list and start to re-define what you really want. Like most people you will be challenged to take your list down to five to seven desires. Again, as you review this list, it is still too long. The time and effort to accomplish these desires still appears to be overwhelming. While you are making progress, your list is too long to get started. And while these desires may reflect what you really want, there are just too many to focus on.

3. Third, the final task is to capture "true" desires, which is to define what you really want and upon which you will act. From your list of five to seven desires choose your top three. These three desires are where your attention is focused and where you will now develop plans to execute them. This will make a "true" difference in your life.

CMAMA ™: a test for evaluating your "true" desires

We all have great intentions. So how do we insure that our intentions line up with our actions? The process of aligning actions with intentions for making and meeting commitments is called CMAMA Tm. This process uses five questions to test for: **Clarity** (to develop clarity on what has been discussed);

Meaningful (to help people better understand why this is important to them); **Achievable** (to help people internalize that they can take control and get what they want); **Measurable** (what gets measured gets done); **Agreed Upon** (the test for commitment to move forward).

The following guide represents questions to be used to evaluate each area of CMAMA:

"A guide to develop more consistent coaching"

1. Clarity
    - What specifically, is the area we are working on?
    - Give me an example of what we are discussing?

2. Meaningful
    - Why would you choose to work on this for your business and/or for yourself?
    - What benefits do you believe you will get from working on this?
    - Why do you believe that this area is important to you and/or your business?

3. Achievable
    - To what extent do you believe that the results are within your control?
    - What will you need to learn to feel that this is achievable?

4. Measurable
    - How would you measure progress on this issue?
    - What benchmarks will you use to evaluate how well you are doing?

- How will you measure your commitment to this task/goal?

5. Agreed Upon
   - On a scale from 1-5, with 1 being low and 5 being high, how committed are you to take action?
   - What one to two things will you do as you leave our session today?

Desire – Choices – Commitments:
The day-to day process for getting what we want

At this point, we have focused our attention on "alignment," capturing "true" desires and the use of CMAMA to evaluate the level of commitment on what will be done. So, what is the process that an individual can use each and every day to make better decisions around these "true" desires? We all have the intention to follow-through, yet there is something that stands in the way in executing what we believe we need to do.

The answer is the choices we make every day on what we do and what we do not do. The key is that we need to learn to link the choices we make to the "true" desires of what it is that we really want. In most cases, we are not conscious or aware of how we make those decisions minute by minute, and day by day and, as result, we get what we deserve which is not necessarily what we want. How may people consciously connect their choices to their desires? When we do this we feel better about ourselves because we are taking action on what we believe/control which is called **Mastery.** Unfortunately, many of us try to take action in areas that we do not control which tends to cause us **Frustration** or even a bit of **Depression,** which is anger turned inward. In other words, we know what to do, but we choose not to do it. We use words like "should have" or "ought to have" done something.

In order to make better choices we need a "**triggering event;**" something that will remind us what to do on a daily basis. We need to take each desire and break it down into the things that must happen to make it a reality. Each person needs to define for him or herself the small steps or the "triggering event" that starts this process. For example, if you had a desire to earn money to fund your child's education there would be certain questions that would need to be asked. Such questions might include: "When will I need the money? How much will I need? How much will I have to earn to put away enough money?" While these are all good questions the key is to define what must happen to "trigger" you to move forward on a daily basis to accomplish this desire. It becomes a domino effect. If you do the daily phoning, you make the appointments and, in turn, develop the clients to earn the money to put away for your child's education. If one of the dominoes is out of sync, the entire process falls apart.

When we link our choices to our desires we can make "true" commitments upon which we can be counted on to deliver. A commitment is a promise that you make to yourself and others that builds your character and integrity. Webster defines a commitment as "…a pledge to do something in the future or a state of being obligated or emotionally impelled." This is a powerful word if we use it in this manner. People are counting on us to follow-through on what we say we will do. How can we expect others to follow-through when they work with us, if we do not follow-through on what we say we will do? Either we live with integrity as demonstrated by our commitments, or we live a life of hypocrisy. There is no middle ground.

41

What would the results be for you if every day each choice you made was connected to the desire you wanted and demonstrated by your commitment to follow-through and take action on? How would you feel about who you are and how others will be attracted to work with you? This fundamental change will change your life!!!

Can you imagine waking up each morning and visualizing these three "true" desires and asking yourself how you will make progress each day in each one, and at the end of the day your only question is, "How much progress did I make within each area of "true" desire?" Think how much better you will feel about yourself and what you are doing each and every day. Instead of feeling overwhelmed, confused, and frustrated, you will focus on what is most important to you. Your commitments will be demonstrated by your actions. You will live a life of fulfillment while unleashing your "true" potential.

"If you are willing to only do
what is easy,
life will be hard.
But if you are willing
to do what's hard,
life will be easy."

-T. Harv Eker

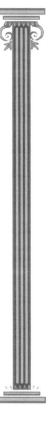

Edward G. Deutschlander, CLU, CLF, has served as Executive Vice President for Minneapolis-based North Star Resource Group since 2002. This year, Ed is President Elect of GAMA International, an organization with over 5,000 individuals who own, manage or operate financial advising firms throughout the world. A main platform speaker at GAMA's annual meeting, LAMP, he spoke to an audience of over 2,000 and was one of only a handful of financial services leaders asked to speak in China, addressing top industry leaders in Beijing, Shanghai, and Hangzhou. In addition, Ed is recognized as the premier recruiter in the financial services industry. Ed has also been published in numerous publications on topics that include recruiting, selection, training and the development of financial advisors. His "Recruiter's Creed" is often used and cited at industry meetings and events. You can reach Ed at 612-617-6103 or ed@northstarfinancial.com

Chapter 3

Be Faithful to What is Helpful

Ed Deutschlander

A very good friend and personal hero of mine, General Agents and Managers Association (GAMA) International Management Hall of Fame inductee, Maury Stewart once shared with me that you might be the only bible someone reads today. Maury also shared with me that someone will see you play for the first time today and everyday, so always be at your best. Bottom-line is that as a leader you are always being watched by those that you lead. Therefore, the most effective way to guide and assist others in reaching their own personal levels of achievement is to practice what you preach and strive each day to reach the levels of achievement you want for yourself.

Observing and studying some of the most successful leaders in the world over the past 20 years, I have noticed some common traits amongst those considered top achievers in all aspects of their lives. This chapter is dedicated to those timeless principles that, if applied, will ensure success. These timeless principles have helped countless others reach their goals in life. We must learn from those who have gone before us and be faithful to what has been helpful.

Self-Discipline—One of the most powerful messages I ever read was in a small booklet titled *The Common Denominator of Success*. In this reprint of a speech delivered in 1940 by Albert Grey, the president of the National Association of Life Underwriters,

45

Grey states that, "Successful people have formed the habits of doing things that 'failures' do not like to do." Nowhere does he say that they enjoy doing those things; they might even dislike doing them more than the 'failures' do. The difference is that they have disciplined themselves to do the very things that most will not do. It comes down to the pain of discipline or the pain of regret. Either way there is pain on the journey to success. The beauty is that we have a choice as to what pain we want to accept. Successful leaders always choose the pain of discipline. They make small promises to themselves each day and they do not break those promises. They tend to plan out the day, doing the most important, challenging and difficult things first. I was instructed early on in life to do the most uncomfortable thing I needed to do each day before 9:00 AM no matter what. I have adhered to this principle almost everyday and can attest that it has been a factor in whatever success I have had.

Values Driven—Achievers' values determine where they will spend their time and resources. Their daily activities are focused on a few critical things that align with their values and goals. If you want to know someone, just observe how they spend their time (the activities they participate in and the company they keep) and where they spend their money (where they allocate their resources). The very best leaders identify their values (why they get up each day and what is important to them), they make decisions based on these values, and they spend their time and resources pursuing these values.

Time Management—Successful leaders maximize their time by making sure they are not wasteful with the most precious resource we have. Time. Watch these individuals; they are always doing something productive and blending their activities. When socializing with a key employee, they are not just having a glass of wine with an employee, they are teaching their employee valuable lessons and concepts and promoting ideas they themselves have learned. They also have the discipline to schedule something and do it. It might be getting up at 5:30 AM to get their daily exercise, or perhaps reading the Bible or meditating. Their motto is—if it gets scheduled, it gets done!

Mentor—The very best leaders have mentors and also serve as mentors. They seek those who have climbed to the very top of the mountain, and they ask them how they did it. They ask them about the mistakes they made on their journey and the things they would have done differently, and they follow their guidance and advice. They know that being a mentor themselves forces them to always be at their best, knowing they are being observed. They also know that when you teach others you learn the subject matter to an even greater degree yourself.

Set Goals—The very best leaders not only set goals but understand the WHY behind the goal. "Why is this goal so important to achieve?" This goes beyond hitting a certain number, objective, income level or recognition. This usually has some deep underlying meaning such as a sense of accomplishment, financial independence, and/or leaving a legacy. We must clearly know why we are doing something, to get through the difficult times that surely lie ahead. Also, create a goal card and have it laminated and carry it with you so you can revisit it several times a day. Carry that goal card with you and "Don't leave home without it!"

Have Daily Critical Numbers—Leaders also know how to measure and monitor their progress towards their goals. *If they can measure it, they can manage it.* They know the critical numbers that need to be hit each day to determine if they're

47

progressing toward their goals or if they need to make adjustments to get back on track. It might be making a certain number of sales calls, obtaining a certain number of referrals, or holding a certain number of meetings. Whatever the number is it can be directly tied to the likelihood of hitting the goal. It is a formula of, "If I do this, then that occurs." When you have measured and monitored your activity to the point where you can detect the ratios and relationships you need, you have identified critical numbers and are on your way to success.

Confront the Brutal Facts—This key principle was best described in the business best seller *Good To Great* by Jim Collins, in which he explains that we must realize that life is indeed difficult and, unfair. And that once this is embraced one can prepare to endure the difficult times and truly enjoy and appreciate the good that occurs in one's life. Also know that there will be times and situations that appear hopeless. One must never lose hope, but realize and accept that there are very difficult situations that lie ahead. Leaders that operate from a mind set of, "What is the worse possible outcome? Am I prepared for that? Can we live with that?" truly put themselves at a competitive advantage to make the changes and adjustments to survive and even thrive in turbulent times.

Lifelong Learners—Leaders learn from just about everything they do. They are constantly observing and asking themselves what they learned in both victory as well as in defeat. From the smallest of observations, like avoiding a certain route to the office knowing it will be backed up with traffic, to big lessons, like why a particular sale succeeded. Leaders take the time to ask why the outcome occurred and what they can do in the future to replicate it or avoid it. They are also voracious readers, knowing that today's readers are tomorrow's leaders.

Practice Makes Perfect—Leaders recognize that nothing should be done without knowing what the likely outcome will be. They rehearse it until they love the outcome. Whether it be preparing for a courageous conversation they will have with an employee who needs to improve his performance, a speech to share the firms new vision, or a simple conversation with a daughter, they go into situations knowing they can control the direction and guide it as best as possible. Winston Churchill, considered to be one of the greatest natural orators, was anything *but* a natural. No one worked harder than he to find the right words to say, and he rehearsed them over and over. Professionals always practice.

Find out What Others Want and Help Them Get There—The very best leaders know that they need to discover what drives and motivates those they lead, and they do everything they can to help their employees reach their goals. From introducing them to a key contact to giving them the chance to share their idea at the upcoming management meeting, the best leaders are always finding ways to grow their people.

Learn a Lot About a Little and Do a Lot of It—The very best leaders know they have to specialize and become an expert in a particular discipline. They master that skill and find opportunities to use it over and over again. Learn as much as possible about a field, topic or discipline and become an expert in that area. Then focus on finding the right situations and markets so you can be that expert all of the time and do it over and over. The very best have mastered this concept and live by it. It is a simple concept but it is a real difference-maker. Learn a lot about a little and do a lot of it!

Deserve to Win Mentality—The best leaders have an unparalleled work ethic. They work hard, not just for the results

49

but for the discipline and mind-set hard work creates. The harder one works the harder it is to give up, or to settle for anything but victory. Rick Pitino, one of the premier National Collegiate Athletic Association basketball coaches in the country, used the following concept with all of his teams. He informed his players that each practice session would be 15 minutes longer than any other Division 1 NCAA team in the country. This was designed so when the game was on the line and when Pitino called a time out in a close game, with seconds remaining, he would remind all of the players that they DESERVED to win because they had practiced longer and harder. When the team members truly feel they deserve something they will do all they can to get it. Creating this mind-set starts with working your hardest. You want your team heading into the final seconds knowing they should win because they earned that right with their hard work. Muhammad Ali once said, "Before I go in the ring, I'd have already won or lost it out on the road. The real part is won or lost somewhere far away from witnesses—behind the lines, in the gym and out there on the road, long before I dance under those lights." The hard work and preparation determines the outcome of the game or event. The scoreboard merely reflects who worked harder preparing.

Always Be a Little Bit Out of Control—Because of his domination as a race car driver, one of my favorite professional athletes is Mario Andretti. When asked his philosophy on why he was so successful he said that he never wanted to feel as if he had complete control over the race car. He always wanted to feel just a lit bit out of control. For him that was the indicator he needed to know that he was pushing himself and getting outside of his comfort zone. The very best leaders embrace this and are never complacent with what they have already accomplished. They recognize that what happened or what was accomplished yesterday doesn't matter. Today is a new day and we need to make it count. Don't count the days but make the days count! Make them count by going a little faster than you think you can while feeling a little bit out of control. Albeit frightening, it should give you the confidence of knowing that you are giving it all you can. Feel good about things being a little bit out of control, it reminds us we are pushing ourselves to the limit.

Live Full, Die Empty—Motivational speaker Les Brown shares this philosophy that the best leaders have embraced. Great leaders know that they must give it everything they have and leave it all on the field in everything they do. They know that it is about always giving it your all, and in the words of world-class runner, Steve Prefontaine, "To give anything but your best is to sacrifice the gift." We were all given the great gift of life itself and to give it your all is the only right thing to do with it.

Pressure vs. Stress—Leaders know the difference between pressure and stress. Pressure is unavoidable. It is a natural element, a part of nature and we live in a natural world. From atmospheric pressure to blood pressure it is part of this world. We must learn to deal with pressure if we are to be successful. There is no escaping it, especially if we are getting out of our comfort zone. Pressure should be viewed as a good thing. It is telling us we are growing. "The car is a little out of control," is our chance to correct the course and regain control. Or, rise to the occasion and grow. The difference between pressure and stress is that the pressure becomes stress when we are not prepared for the situation. Pressure is the upcoming speaking engagement. But we have rehearsed hundreds of times and are anxious and excited because we are prepared and know we will do well and know it will be a break-through moment for us. This only becomes stress when we have not prepared adequately and we know that, but we *hope* all goes well. Hope

51

is a wonderful thing but I learned a long time ago it is a lousy strategy. We should not hope things go well due to lack of discipline. We should hope and expect things to go well because we are prepared. Leaders learn to be prepared for the many pressure-filled situations they will face, and make them growth opportunities that will get them to new heights. Embrace pressure with the discipline of practice and see how quickly you can grow.

Provide More Service Than You Get Paid For—One of the biggest challenges we have today is living in a world of instant gratification. People want to receive their payment before providing a service. Not only is that backwards thinking but successful leaders recognize that you should deliver even more than what you are paid for. I have heard the phrase, "Under promise, over deliver." I do not completely agree with that. Never under-promise, and be careful what you do promise, as you must always fulfill those promises. When you do make a promise simply provide more. Leaders and businesses that do this are the ones that create legacies and set the bar for new standards. Every time you have a chance to deliver, deliver more and see just what happens!

Leader First, Friend Second—The best leaders know and understand that they need to be leaders first. They have an obligation to those they lead; whether it be as a parent with their children or the CEO of their firm. One must be a leader first—only then can they transition to a friend. The all time winningest NCAA basketball coach, Bobby Knight, once shared his philosophy about coaching and raising children. He stated that an often made mistake is that parents and coaches try to be their kids' friends *first* and parents and coaches second. If that occurs, you end up being a parent and coach the rest of your life. If you are their parent and coach *first,* you end up becoming their friend the rest of your life. This is very true, and the very best leaders know that leadership is doing what needs to be done and not necessarily what the person wants to have done.

Four Rules of Business—Life Insurance Industry legend Al Granum taught this to me and it's simple but speaks volumes, and those that think in this manner truly put themselves at a competitive advantage to make the changes and adjustments to survive and even thrive in turbulent times. (1) Keep your promises—be careful about making promises for this very reason, (2) Be five minutes early to everything, (3) Finish the job you start, (4) Say Please and Thank you (be polite at all times). Excuses do not fix anybody's neglect of anything!

Do Things the Right Way First—All too often we want to change things and customize them immediately. Whether it is the way we want to hold a golf club, or trying a cooking recipe. What we need to do is do things right, the way they were meant to be done, first and master that technique before we customize. The very best painters all mastered the fundamentals before they went on to become expressionists. They knew the laws and fundamentals of painting before moving on to their own variations. This allowed them to teach others. The best leaders insist that someone learn the right way, or the company way, before creating their own way. Here's a phrase we coined—*one earns independence through performance.* The athletes, who master the fundamentals and demonstrate this by getting results on the field, earn the coach's confidence that they can make adjustments based on their own discretion. This must be earned through mastering the fundamentals. As someone becomes better and more proficient doing something the right way, they have earned the ability to create their own style.

CEO— is the Chief Evangelist Officer. CEO's are the Chief Evangelist Officers inside of the company. They must preach and teach the vision, mission and values. If it is important to you it will become important to others. You must really own it and believe in it. The best leaders know this and are passionate about their causes and live each day with purpose. In Og Mandino's classic The Greatest Salesman in the World, one of the ten scrolls states that, "Never will I forget that many have attained great wealth and success with only one sales talk, delivered with Excellence." This is being passionate about one's purpose, believing in the vision, mission and cause, and getting others energized about this as well. They know that the days are numbered and they maximize each one. Today is a gift, thus the reason it is called the PRESENT. The leader's role is to energize others toward the purpose and mission of the group. The only way this can be done is to be the Chief Evangelist Officer.

Anything Done With Pride and Effort Becomes Noble—Any task one does, regardless of how small it is, becomes noble if it is done with pride and effort. Leaders know this and apply it at all times. They treat everything as if it were important because it is important to someone. Some examples include making sure you attend a function if you were invited, as it means a lot to those who invited you. When asked to share a few words, realize the impact you can make. Take pride in knowing that everything you do in life has your good name stamped all over it. Teach this to your children and those you lead. Some of the most respected people in organizations do not necessarily have the biggest incomes or fanciest titles, but they still take incredible pride in everything they do. Service Master built an entire cleaning empire around this concept. The Service Master employee cleaning the hospital floor knows they play an important part of the healing process for that patient. Having a clean environment protects one from infection and provides peace of mind. Do everything you take on, with all your spirit, and as if your name were stamped on it!

TRUST—The greatest leaders know that trust must not be violated. This is what everyone expects and wants from their leaders; to know they can trust them. This must happen: to be forthright and truthful even when it might be painful. Leaders know that it is better to be honest and deal with the issues and their aftermath than to be deceitful to protect someone's feelings. Deceit will cause the loss of trust. If trust is gained, then the discipline and love to improve and grow people can be extended to make everyone better.

I was at a crossroad in my life when I wrote the following. I needed some time to reflect and figure out just who I was and what I wanted to become. This has served me well over the years, and I want to share it with you.

In order to remain faithful to my personal philosophies, moral and ethical codes, there is only one way for me to conduct myself and that is to demand and expect excellence.

In whatever challenges or situations that I encounter which require my attention and focus, it is at that time I must respond with intense and thoughtful preparation and effort.

It is through this determination and professionalism and constant prioritizing that I will achieve my goals, and more importantly encompass the attributes needed to become a better person who will only stand for personal improvement on a continual and life-long basis. It is from all of this that my most important goal will be reached, and that is that through my own actions I inspire all the wonderful, loving individuals who have come into my life to expect only the best from themselves, which will eventually make them better in some aspect of their lives—making a difference.

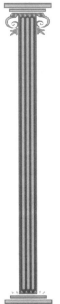

Machen MacDonald, CPCC, CCSC is the creator of The Power of Coaching book series, the founder of the ProBrilliance Leadership Institute, and a full time certified business and personal coach. With over 15 years of experience in the financial services industry, he's now a full time coach dedicated to showing business leaders how to provoke their brilliance so they can experience their ideal life. He's an accomplished author, as well as a highly sought after speaker for his dynamic and unique perspectives on achieving success in all areas of life. Machen resides on his ranch in Northern California with his wife and their three children.

Contact Machen at (530)273-8000 or email him at: machen@probrilliance.com.

Chapter 4

Business Plans Made Easy—Get it on One Page

Machen P. MacDonald

Simple clear purpose in principle gives rise to complex intelligent behavior. Complex rules and regulations give rise to simple and stupid behavior. — Dee Hock

If that is so then your business plan must be only one page. Now, wait a minute! I can already hear your limiting beliefs crop up. The committee inside your head is attempting to get you to believe things like: "A business plan on only one page can't be done. It couldn't possibly capture everything my business is about and where we are headed. My manager(s) or VP(s) wouldn't take it or me seriously. My banker would laugh at me." Au contraire.

Be careful here; as leadership and management expert Eugene Taurman so eloquently states, "What you see depends on what you thought before you looked."

When it comes to business plans, most entrepreneurs and sales people slip into a low grade coma anticipating the exercises of creating vision and mission statements. Heck, go ask 10 experts what the difference is between a vision and mission statement and you get 12 different answers.

It's no wonder we can all relate to the following definition:

A mission statement is defined as *"a long awkward sentence that demonstrates management's inability to think clearly."* All good companies have one.

—From The Dilbert Principle, 1996

You see the exercise of gaining clarity and eliminating the fluff and fat is the key. You must become crystal-clear and hold daily, in the forefront, your vision of what you are ultimately trying to accomplish. We can't become what we want to be by remaining what we are. It is going to take some time, thought-energy and work. However, you have a choice here. You can either make it drudgery or you can be inspired by the process. Again, it's your choice. Choose wisely.

Your brain works faster than you think. You only need to have clarity around 5 elements with regards to your business and your plan.

1. What are you trying to accomplish?
2. Why does your business exist?
3. What results will you measure?
4. How will you build or grow this company?
5. What is the work to be done?

That's pretty simple right? Sure, though it's not necessarily easy. It may take some brainstorming and a couple of drafts but you can do it! This single endeavor of getting a business plan down on one page has lead thousands of businesses in hundred of industries to achieve dramatic results.

Once you are clear on what business you are building (your vision) and you understand and are inspired by why your business exists (your mission) then and only then can you be clear on what objectives will carry out your mission and manifest your vision. Your key objectives, which must be measurable and graph-able, can only be executed through clearly defined completion-oriented strategies.

So far so good. I am starting to sense some light bulbs turning on out there. Now we must drop down from the 10,000 foot level on to the runway. If we don't know what actions are necessary to carry out the strategies then what good is the plan or the planning process? Good question.

The action plan section of your business plan defines the work that must be done and specifically by *when*. These are the key links in order to carry out the key strategies to support the objective of *what* you are trying to accomplish by bending your sales curve.

A vision without a task is only hallucination.
An action without a vision is a nightmare.
Vision & action together is inspiration to serve the world.

Remember you have four quarters in a year so don't load everything into the upcoming quarter and subject yourself to overwhelm. Spread it out over four quarters. Keep this in mind—time exists so everything doesn't have to happen all at once. Think! Plan! And get it on one page.

Go easy on yourself and don't think you have to write the perfect plan. The important thing is to get your plan in writing, even if it's not perfect. Strive for the high standard of Excellence! Your business plan is a working document and will never really be done. Things come up. Life happens. You will need to recalibrate your plan throughout the year, and that's okay.

So don't just DO something, sit there! Get perspective and reflect rather than just continuing to do the same thing and getting the same results. Once you have thought it out, capture it on one page. This will provide you the clarity and the courage to go forth and serve your clients and those you lead in the most authentic way.

It's like Mario Andretti says, "If things seem really under control, you're not going fast enough." So go BIG and capture on one page how you are going to make this your best year yet! For a sample One Page Business Plan® see page 62.

Here are some provocative questions and inside insights to get you started in formulating your One Page Business Plan ®.

- **Vision Statement**: *What are we building?*

   Inside Insight: This typically describes what the business will look like in three or five years. Be sure to include the answers to: What are the company's products and services? What markets will we serve? What will the dimensions of the company be?

- **Mission Statement**: *Why are we building it?*

   Inside Insight: This should be timeless. The more concise the better. Try and get your mission statement under eight words. This describes why the business exists from the point of view of the customer. Be sure to include what we provide that is unique. What is our competitive edge in the market? Give some thought to what we want to be known for.

- **Objective**: *What are the results we want to measure this year?*

Inside Insight: Make sure our objectives are S.M.A.R.T. (Specific, Measurable, Actionable, Relevant and Time-Bound). Ultimately we will want to create a scorecard for each of our objectives, so our objective should be easy to graph. List five to nine goals that this business must achieve to be successful. Some categories to consider are: What are the vital monthly, quarterly statistics that we can track this year and compare year over year? What are the causal factors in generating the results we are looking for?

- **Strategy:** *How are we going to build this business over time?*

  Inside Insight: Describe five to eight things that this business must do well over time to be successful. Key things to consider: How will we attract/retain clients? How will we promote our products & services? What will differentiate us from our competitors? How will we use technology? What types of strategic alliances will we form? Why? What type of culture will we encourage? What is our exit strategy?

- **Action Plans:** *What are the six to eight specific business building projects we must successfully COMPLETE this year?- or- What is the work to be done?*

  Inside Insight: Name the projects, with action verbs, we need to work on this year and identify who is going to do what by when. What is the result we want to achieve with each project?

Special Inside Insight: In coaching, we know that what we focus on expands. The questioning process above helps you to gain clarity with regard to what you are building and why you are building it. Then, you can identify what work needs to be done and how. By creating a One Page Plan, you are creating a resource that is ubiquitous and will assure you focus your focus on what you want to bring about. This in and of itself will pay you and those you lead more dividends than anything else you could do.

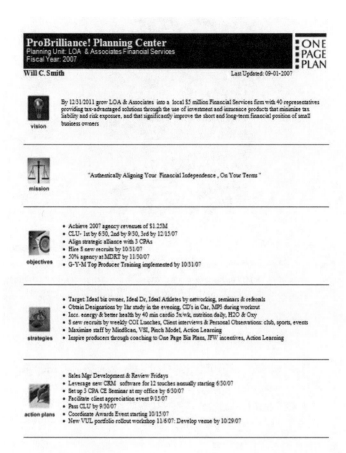

ProBrilliance! Planning Center
Planning Unit: LOA & Associates Financial Services
Fiscal Year: 2007

ONE PAGE PLAN

Will C. Smith

Last Updated: 09-01-2007

vision — By 12/31/2011 grow LOA & Associates into a local $5 million Financial Services firm with 40 representatives providing tax-advantaged solutions through the use of investment and insurance products that minimize tax liability and risk exposure, and that significantly improve the short and long-term financial position of small business owners

mission — "Authentically Aligning Your Financial Independence, On Your Terms"

objectives
- Achieve 2007 agency revenues of $1.25M
- CLU- 1st by 6/30, 2nd by 9/30, 3rd by 12/15/07
- Align strategic alliance with 3 CPAs
- Hire 8 new recruits by 10/31/07
- 50% agency at MDRT by 11/30/07
- G-Y-M Top Producer Training implemented by 10/31/07

strategies
- Target: Ideal biz owner, Ideal Dr, Ideal Athletes by networking, seminars & referrals
- Obtain Designations by 1hr study in the evening, CD's in Car, MP3 during workout
- Incr. energy & better health by 40 min cardio 3x/wk, nutrition daily, H2O & Oxy
- 8 new recruits by weekly COI Lunches, Client interviews & Personal Observations: club, sports, events
- Maximize staff by MindScan, VSI, Pinch Model, Action Learning
- Inspire producers through coaching to One Page Biz Plans, JFW incentives, Action Learning

action plans
- Sales Mgr Development & Review Fridays
- Leverage new CRM software for 12 touches annually starting 6/30/07
- Set up 3 CPA CE Seminar at my office by 6/30/07
- Facilitate client appreciation event 9/15/07
- Pass CLU by 9/30/07
- Coordinate Awards Event starting 10/15/07
- New VUL portfolio rollout workshop 11/6/07: Develop venue by 10/29/07

The One Page Business Plan ® is a registered trademark of The One Page Business Plan Company.

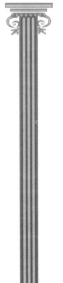

Denis Waitley is a respected author, keynote speaker and productivity consultant on high performance human achievement. The following article was reproduced with permission from Denis Waitley's Weekly Ezine.

To subscribe to Denis Waitley's Weekly Ezine, go to www.deniswaitley.com or send an email with the word "Join" in the subject line to subscribe@deniswaitley.com

Reproduced with permission from Denis Waitley's Weekly Ezine.

Chapter 5

From Motivation to Motive-Action

Denis Waitley

With the passing of every new year each of us needs to understand the magnitude of social and economic change in the world. In the past, change in business and social life was incremental and a set of personal strategies for achieving excellence was not required. Today, in the knowledge-based world, where change is the rule, a set of personal strategies is essential for success, even survival. Never again will you be able to go to your place of business on autopilot, comfortable and secure that the organization, state or government will provide for and look after you. You must look in the mirror when you ask who is responsible for your success or failure. You must become a lifelong learner and leader, for to be a follower is to fall hopelessly behind the pace of progress. The power brokers in the new global arena will be the knowledge facilitators. Ignorance will be even more the tyrant and enslaver than in the past. As you look in the mirror to see the 21st Century you, there will also be another image standing beside you. It is your competition. Your competition, from now on, will be a hungry immigrant with a wireless, hand-held, digital assistant. Hungry for food, hungry for a home, for a new car, for security, for a college education. Hungry for knowledge. Smart, quick thinking, skilled and willing to do anything necessary to be competitive in the world marketplace. Working long hours and Saturdays, staying open later, serving customers better and more cheerfully. To be a player in the 21st Century you have to be willing to give more in service than you receive in payment.

These are the new rules in the game of life. These are the actions you must take to be a leader and a winner in your personal and professional life. By mastering these profoundly simple action steps, you will be positioned to be a change master in the new century.

Action Step Number One - Consider Yourself Self-Employed, But Be a Team Player. What this means is that you are your own Chief Executive Officer of your future. Start thinking of yourself as a service company with a single employee. You're a small company that puts your services to work for a larger company. Tomorrow you may sell those services to a different organization, but that doesn't mean you're any less loyal to your current employer. Taking responsibility for yourself in this way does mean that you never equate your personal long-term interests with your employer's.

The first idea is resolving not to suffer the fate of those who lost their jobs and found their skills were obsolete. The second is to begin immediately the process of protecting yourself against that possibility – by becoming proactive instead of reactive.

Ask yourself these questions: How vulnerable am I? What trends must I watch? What information must I gain? What knowledge do I lack?

Again, think of yourself as a company. Set up a training department in your mind and make certain your top employee is updating his or her skills. Make sure you have your own private pension plan, knowing that you are responsible for your own financial security.

Entrusting the government or an employer, other than yourself, with your retirement income is like hiring a compulsive gambler as your accountant.

You're the CEO of your daily life who must have the vision to set your goals and allocate your resources. The mindset of being responsible for your own future used to be crucial only to the self-employed, but it has become essential for us all. Today's typical employees are no longer one-career people. Most will have five separate careers in their lifetimes. Remember, your competition is a hungry immigrant with a laptop. Action Step Number One is to consider yourself to be self-employed, but be a team player.

Action Step Number Two - Be Flexible in the Face of Daily Surprises. We live in a time-starved, overstressed, violent society. Much of our over-reaction to what happens to us every day is a result of our self-indulgent value system, where we blame others for our problems, look to organizations or the government for our solutions, thirst for immediate sensual gratification and believe we should have privileges without responsibilities. This condition is manifested in the high crime rate and in the increase in violence in the work place where employees blame their managers for threatening their security.

I have learned how to be flexible in the face of daily surprises, which is one of the most important action traits for a leader. I really haven't been angry for about 17 years. During that time, no one has tried to physically harm me or someone close to me. I've learned to adapt to stress in life and reserve my fear or anger for imminently physically dangerous situations. I rarely, if ever, get upset with what people say, do or don't do, even if it inconveniences me. I do react emotionally when I see someone physically or emotionally abusing or victimizing another. But I've learned not to sweat the small stuff.

The Serenity Prayer, "Grant me the Serenity to accept the things I cannot change, the Courage to change the things I can, and the Wisdom to know the difference" is a valuable measuring tool we can apply to our lives. Simple yet profound words to live by.

> "Happiness is a
> conscious choice,
> not an
> automatic response."
>
> - Mildred Barthel

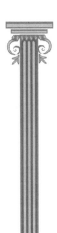

Brett Bauer is the owner of Bauer Capital Management, a wealth advisory firm in Eden Prairie, MN. Brett has been in the insurance and securities business for nearly 20 years. At Bauer Capital, he works primarily with high income, high net worth, self-employed individuals. His team of experts at Bauer Capital provides allows their clients to "get it all" from their firm. Brett and Bauer Capital are affiliated with Woodbury Financial Services of Woodbury, MN. Brett can be reached by email at brett@bauercap.com.

Rich Campe graduated as a Certified Coach with Tony Robbins and is part of the Jim Rohn International Coaching team. A very successful business owner and entrepreneur, his real passion lies in helping people reach their true potential. Rich's clients include Bank of America, Northwestern Mutual, AXA, Ameriprise, and Planco. Rich resides in Charlotte, NC, with his lovely wife, Catherine, and their two children, Camden and Lawson. For more information, visit his website at www.richcampe.com. To contact Rich, send an email to info@richcampe.com or telephone 704-752-7760.

Chapter 6

Is Your Ladder Leaning Against The Right Wall?

A real life coaching journey with Brett Bauer (Successful Advisor and Coaching Client) and Rich Campe (Professional Coach and founder of RCI Corporate and Personal Coaching)

<u>**The Client Perspective**</u> with Brett Bauer – Independent Financial Advisor and Owner of Bauer Capital Management

In June of 2006, I had already produced over $1 Million Dollars in gross commissions. My business at that point was primarily a transaction based business and was focused solely on completing deals. I was paid very well, worked very hard and enjoyed the fruits of my labor. I invested in the deals I sold and assumed a high degree of risk by participating in these venture capital investments. I was satisfied and happy with life at the time. However, I realized that once a deal was done the fulfillment was gone. It also dawned on me that the business was totally dependant upon me. I couldn't leave the office and know that things would get done. I was no longer working on the business; I was a slave to the business.

When I realized that sad truth, I set out to do something about it. I called the president of the broker dealer where I worked and asked what he would think if I were to reinvest in my business and in the process "reinvent my business" so that I

71

would be able build a more scaleable business and focus on what I loved to do, which was work with companies raising money and connecting them with investors. He told me that the best time for me to implement a change like that was while I was at the top of my game and performing well, so that I could steer my own course, as opposed to waiting until I was forced to make a change.

With that in mind, I was fortunate to meet Rich Campe, who has become my personal coach. This transforming process allowed me to discover my true motivations, learn more about my strengths and weaknesses and caused me to facilitate a plan that squeezed ten years of goals into a two to three year time frame.

I actually tried coaching back in 1999. I knew a million dollar producer at a firm who used a personal coach to run his business. I assumed that if it worked for him that invariably it would work for me as well. I retained the services of a coach so that I, too, could become a million dollar producer, but I discovered that there was little structure and no accountability. We talked on a weekly basis, but there was no attempt on my part or the coach's to design a plan. I wanted to be successful, but had no idea what kind of outcome I was looking for.

The Rich Campe International (RCI) coaching program is different because it has structure, time-tested principles, accountability and scientific research to support the results. RCI has the meat, not just the sizzle. If someone has studied successful advisors and they can share the results of the research and apply this to my business, sign me up. Success leaves clues and I want the clues.

I heard that Rich is the "Tony Robbins" of the financial services industry. I'm not superhuman—I'm just a normal guy—and I felt that if Rich could help me he could help anyone. I hoped he would help me articulate specific results that I wanted to achieve and reinforce strengths that I possess.

When I initially completed my *MindScan*™ I was skeptical about the information that could be gleaned from the types of questions they asked, the ordering of the information and the fact that it took only twenty minutes to complete. I failed to understand how the questions that were asked could reveal some deep level of inner psyche or provide insight. The thing that stood out to me was that the extreme responses in the *MindScan*™ were easy and that the middle portion of the *MindScan*™ was perplexing because it was difficult to rank seemingly similar bad events. I remember thinking while taking the test; I have to choose between a mad bomber or a man carrying a bomb. The results were revealing and intriguing.

I had seven main objectives that I wanted to accomplish by entering into Rich's coaching program;

Professionally:
• Continue to learn, grow my business, double or triple my production in 12-18 months
• Outsource and hire staff, and free up my time
• Build a business that creates lasting value that ultimately could be sold

Personally:
• Be a better husband and father, and spend more time with my family
• Get in better physical condition

- Play more golf and lower my handicap
- Take some time off, be a better human being, and have more balance in my life

I was interviewed for our company newsletter regarding my coaching with Rich, and asked why I wanted to share my personal experience with the coaching process. I had already thought about the question so the answer was easy. I wanted to help other reps. I said, "If more reps knew where I started, how I got it together, and how I got to where I am, there would be more Crystal Qualifiers, the top 1%. I put my pants on the same way everyone else does, one leg at a time. There is no magic. If I can double my production, anyone can. The first step is that you have to believe that you can. I want to help give them belief."

Although I had doubts that the *MindScan*™ could delve into my psyche and reveal intriguing information, I was surprised by the results. It confirmed a number of things for me, and highlighted potential blind spots.

My *MindScan*™ said that, I have outstanding clarity with regards to being aware of people and their emotions, and relate well and trust easily. It also said I have a tendency to put people into incorrect positions because I align them according to the potential that I see in them, EVEN THOUGH they may not see it themselves. It said I am a rescuer and don't allow others to do their work because I feel I can do it better, faster and easier.

The *MindScan*™ also revealed that:
- I've been experiencing "Role Frustration." The business was successful but I didn't feel successful or productive. I was working too many hours, my wife, Danelle, was

undergoing a kidney transplant and our son, Jack was having multiple eye surgeries. My frustration: The business stops when I'm not there.

- I tend to disregard myself by putting others first.
- I don't like to be compared to others.

Rich had me complete:

- "My Big Game," (my goals for the year)
- "Smart Outcomes," (steps to turn my goals into reality)
- A "Three Tier Purpose Statement" for each goal

I answered questions like: (1) What am I doing to deserve this outcome? (2) What more could I be doing? (3) What resources can I leverage? The answers helped us design a score card and set core activities to track my progress.

Completing these exercises was not easy. I occasionally got frustrated because I wanted to get on with achieving the goals. Being specific was a challenge and my inclination was to fight the process. Still, Rich and I talked weekly and I completed all the tasks. Eventually I found the exercises energizing.

My "Big Game" is to:

- Generate $2.5 million GDC by the end of 2007 and position my practice for sale
- Have more family time
- Play golf and generate new business by leveraging my golf club membership
- Establish a charitable foundation to help prevent drug and alcohol abuse in children, help fund a cure for diabetes and educate children about other cultures

Once we completed the above, I set out to recreate my business so that I could accomplish all of the objectives outlined above.

The Big Game has been the *catalyst for change*. Here are some of the things we've accomplished:

- Transitioned to a wealth advisory-based platform
- Purchased a new office building
- Expanded the team to include an operations manager and a client relations manager working with wholesalers and vendors
- Developed a proprietary business model (with remote access to all tools) to increase productivity and profitability, while allowing us to recruit reps
- Invested $40,000 in computer servers, workstations, software, and a state-of-the-art phone system that's expandable to 75 users
- Purchased Peak Performance systematization tools
- Developed company intranet
- Established and enhanced referral relationships
- Developed internal processes
- Prepared a 20-page business plan that includes historical financials, breakeven analysis and sales forecasts
- Attended Peter Montoya's branding seminar and retained a company to assist us with our marketing efforts
- Created a turnkey, compliance approved document program to use in the Wealth Advisory Process which includes documents and scripts for every stage in the process with the ultimate goal of enabling the client complete the process in fifteen business days

This scratches only the surface. To sum it all up: the growth strategy has gone from a business based on my production to one based on my production *and* the production of other reps

76

who join Bauer Capital Management. In essence, I'm spending more time working on the business instead of always working in the business. I'm really moving from a self-employed model to a big-business model.

I have learned to:

- Be patient
- Be accountable
- Align my goals with personal motivation. If there is no emotional connection, the goals are meaningless
- Check my progress

I am reminded of a story I once read of a hard charging, career driven executive. He was striving so hard to be successful that shortly after achieving his dream he discovered that what he thought he wanted was—in no way—what he had achieved. He was driven by the achievement of a single goal, the office of the chief executive. When he accomplished his goal, it in no way resembled the idea he held of what it should be. The warning here was to be careful before you attempt to climb that "ladder of success." You might discover that the ladder was leaning against the wrong wall.

Early in my career I secured an appointment with one of the most successful individuals in the town I grew up in. Upon entering his office, I saw a picture on his wall that impacted me then and still holds the same meaning for me. It was simply a picture of three seagulls in flight, the caption on the picture read, "They can, because they think they can."

Finally, I learned in Alcoholics Anonymous about the definition of insanity: Thinking the same way you have always thought and expecting a different result.

It was one of the things that helped me quit drinking. It is also something I see quite often; advisors who are trying to do the same old thing, and expecting a different result.

As Bob Dylan once said, "The times they are a changing."

The Coach Perspective with Rich Campe – Professional Coach and founder of RCI Corporate and Personal Coaching

To be candid, when Brett Bauer approached me about the opportunity to work with him, I was both excited and a bit reluctant. You see, our coaching model is designed to move Advisors and Entrepreneurs towards doubling their personal income in 12 months or less. Up to this point, most of our clients were producing $50,000 to $400,000 in personal annual income. Brett was different in that he was already an extremely successful Advisor / Entrepreneur, producing over $1 million in 2005. To top it off, his Broker Dealer asked to track the progress throughout the year and share the results with all their Advisors company-wide. Like many of my clients, I was wrestling with my own limiting beliefs. Could we actually pull off doubling Brett's income? Practicing what I preach, I worked with my coach to replace these limiting beliefs with new empowering ones and decided to move forward with the partnership.

The track Brett and I would run on is called the *Advisor 7 Secrets*™, RCI's proprietary coaching model based on years of researching best practices of Advisors with annual incomes in excess of $500,000. The *Advisor 7 Secrets* ™ include:

Secret 1 – Self Awareness and Outcome Clarity Solution
Secret 2 – Leverage Momentum Strategy
Secret 3 – Perpetual Success Conditioning
Secret 4 – Value Specific Identity
Secret 5 – Strategic Alliance Acceleration
Secret 6 – Processes, People and Systems Synergy
Secret 7 – Succession and Legacy Abundant Living

* For more detail on RCI's *Advisor 7 Secrets* ™ - *Secret 1*, refer to Appendix 1 at the end of this chapter.

I can still remember our first coaching call on October 16, 2006. Brett was ready for the challenge, playing full out! Knowing how critical this is to the client's success, I was really encouraged. Brett was willing to take ownership, be accountable, be real and be coached. He was totally committed to realizing his true potential.

Starting with Secret 1, *Self Awareness and Outcome Clarity Solution*, we began the process utilizing RCI's proprietary *MindScan*™ thinking assessment designed to uncover the thinking behind an individual's attitudes, personality, habits, behaviors and ultimate results. Because everything starts with our thinking, this is the key to unlocking a person's greatest potential. Through Brett's *MindScan*™ results, we were able to identify his thinking strengths, potential weaknesses and patterns in his thinking. In other words, we were able to see ways to accelerate the results and eliminate obstacles which may hinder them.

With this foundational understanding, we developed a plan that would combine powerful coaching strategies with the remaining Secrets to create incredible momentum towards Brett's new exciting "Big Game" goal. Again, it all started with his thinking, and with over 700,000 *MindScan*™ reports to date. I'm still amazed at its accuracy and immense value in the coaching process.

What we learned from Brett's *MindScan*™, as illustrated in Appendix 2 at the end of this Chapter, is that Brett really cared so much about people that he would likely put them in roles just because he sees so much of their potential, and not necessarily because they demonstrated the right fit for it. This is illustrated in the *MindScan*™ by his external world view of *people* being the area he values the most (the highest point of the three external world dimensions). With that information we quickly reviewed the players on his team and made the appropriate changes.

We further realized Brett was experiencing frustration in his roles and not feeling like he was being all he could be, which was showing up in the areas of "role awareness" and "self-esteem" within the "internal world" of the *MindScan*™ results graph. This may seem surprising based on his earning over $1 million in personal income but it's not unusual. Sometimes in life we come to realize our ladder was placed against the wrong wall and we may have to climb down in order to place it against the right wall and climb up again to a higher level. Think about it; how often do we actually take the time to define our Purpose, Vision, Mission and "Big Game" in life? These introspective tools allow us to identify our own wall rather than one that external forces influenced us to climb.

So, after defining Brett's BIG GAME, it was clear his ladder was against a wall that wasn't aligned with his overall purpose and in order to move his ladder, he had to climb down. This is usually where most of us are not willing to go, though a very necessary part of achieving extraordinary results. It's like Brett says, "Insanity is doing the same thing over and over and expecting different results." The wall Brett had his ladder against was the self-employed slave model and not the wall of Big Business. In order for Brett to fulfill his purpose of spending more time with his family and being actively involved with chartable organizations for kids, he would need to climb down the ladder on which he was standing.

This ladder moving business can be very scary which is why coaching plays such a critical role. After all, FEAR is the most common obstacle for reaching our greatest potential. We don't like to let go of what's familiar and comfortable to grab hold of something new. I had to remind Brett the definition of F.E.A.R. is False Evidence Appearing Real. At first he was not ready to make this move but after several calls of clarifying his purpose and aligning his belief systems it happened! Brett was ready to climb down to move his life and business to a new level. His "Why" of serving others like his family and children became HUGE.

At this point it was like opening up the heavens. It was amazing how fast Brett began climbing down his ladder to move it and start climbing up a new wall. Frankly, I had trouble keeping up with him at times. This is such a key component of understanding ones strengths, managing ones potential weaknesses and having total clarity about the ladder we're using and the wall we're climbing. When the WHY at the

81

top of the ladder becomes so compelling, we climb much more rapidly and with much greater joy and zeal.

Back to the *MindScan*™ for a moment—one thing that is really amazing about it is that we can re-examine our thinking after 3 – 12 months to see how we're thinking differently. In other words, have we managed our thinking in ways that have enabled new, more empowering, patterns to develop? Have we, in fact, changed our thinking at the core level?

We could see by Brett's updated *MindScan*™ taken on 6/3/07 (about 10 months after the initial *MindScan*™) that his thinking was clearly aligned with his purpose and he was taking massive action to climb up this new, inspiring ladder of personal and business success (illustrated in the Appendix by his large circle of clarity in his internal world of the *"Role Awareness"* and his large circle of clarity in the area of *"Practical Thinking"*). This meant Brett had total clarity about what could be done and what he could do to make it happen. We also noticed that his clarity in *"Practical Thinking"* was now the highest area of value in his external world, even surpassing his high value of people (illustrated by the fact that *"Practical Thinking"* is the highest of all three dimensions within the external world). This meant Brett was taking MASSIVE ACTION to get down the ladder he was on, and up the new one leaning on a higher wall with a better view!

Whenever we coaches see these powerful shifts and transitions happening, we know to be on the lookout for new areas of potential thinking weaknesses showing up in the *MindScan*™ results. Brett's clarity in *"Structured Thinking"* had decreased while at the same time he was seeing less value in having a detailed plan. This meant Brett was coming up with a plethora of ideas and wanting to implement them all yesterday. While this is amazing, great stuff, if we take massive action without some planning and structure around it, we can find ourselves jumping from one great idea to another without the focus on the core activities needed to reach the top. By using a Score Card, we were able to keep the critical successes and subsequent actions in full view and focus so this creative energy would compliment rather than distract Brett from the core action items needed to achieve his desired outcomes. Once again, this is where coaching is invaluable. With this powerful tracking and measuring tool in place, we were both reading from the same page and I was able to hold him accountable for his plan.

I have no doubt that Brett will reach the incredible new heights he's aiming for, and living the life of purpose he deserves with his ladder of success well positioned against the RIGHT wall. Rock on, Brett!

We MUST learn to maximize our strengths and manage our potential weaknesses. This starts by understanding our thinking at a core level.

To receive a free sample MindScan™ of one of your natural strengths, go to:
www.richcampe.com/powerofcoaching

User ID: powerofcoaching
Password: success

Appendix I

Secret #1
Self-Awareness and Outcome Clarity Solutions

Now, we're going to let you in on a little secret: These secrets aren't really secrets at all! They are finely honed, well cultivated thinking and business strategies that are sculpted to fit your business, your customers and most importantly, the best of who you are.

That's why the first "secret" is focused on understanding who you really are and what you really want from your life and business. Your coach will lead you through a non-judgmental process to achieve the following objectives:

o   Identify your strengths and how to leverage them to achieve your God given potential.
o   Increase awareness around the weaknesses and blind-spots holding you back.
o   Create a vision and sense of purpose for your life and profession.
o   Reframe life's opportunities into a "Game" that's winnable and enjoyable.
o   Develop a personal Scorecard to establish, track and measure intention towards your goals.

Your coach will help you to apply one of the most proven and essential principles of successful living, the ability to fully leverage your strengths while managing your weaknesses and blind spots through the art of awareness, boundaries and delegating what you can to those who compliment you with their abilities.

To illustrate this point, consider a football coach. The first thing the coach will do is carefully evaluate each and every member of the team, increasing awareness of each player's strengths and weaknesses. Based on this awareness, the coach will then decide what positions will maximize their strengths and minimize their weaknesses to ultimately create the right synergy and "chemistry" for a winning team. Have you ever seen a Super Bowl team where the quarterback was also the kicker? No way!

Life is a "team sport." We cannot play the game of life by ourselves. As quarterbacks in our own lives, we must identify the strengths of others and create ways to find synergy in order to win the game of life. Don't assume because you don't have employees this principle doesn't apply to you. It does! You just have to be creative. Your coach will be instrumental in this effort and it all begins with self-awareness and defining your "game!"

By the end of Secret 1, you will have the foundation for propelling your life and business to dizzying new heights. So, let's get started!!

Appendix II

07/26/06

Brett Bauer's THINKING OVERVIEW GF

MindScan taken on 06/04/2007 09:43:52
Your Perspective of the World and Yourself

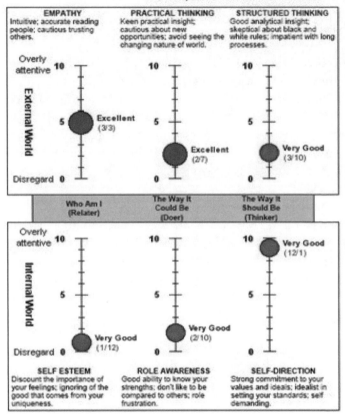

Evidence
Coaching Works!

06/03/07

Brett Bauer's THINKING OVERVIEW GF

MindScan taken on 06/03/2007 16:20:05
Your Perspective of the World and Yourself

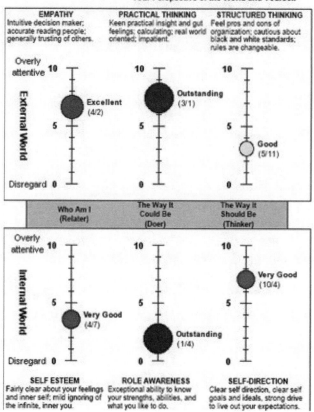

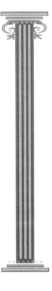 Diane M. Ruebling is the President of The Ruebling Group LLC, a company that provides executive coaching, business planning and performance systems. In addition to her professional career, Diane has held a variety of public service roles. The most current is a Presidential appointment to the Board of Directors for the Overseas Private Investment Corporation (OPIC). She is married to her husband, Charles, and has two children. To contact Diane, email her at diane@rueblinggroup.com or telephone her at 801-520-6761. To find out more about the Ruebling Group, visit their website at www.rueblinggroup.com.

Chapter 7

EMOTIONAL COMPETENCE :
The Path To Achievement and Success!

Diane M. Ruebling

Success in today's fast paced, competitive, and change oriented world creates a demand, more than ever, for people who are emotionally competent. Organizations want people who can thrive in chaos, handle stress, and lead others to higher levels of performance.

It is easy to see that some people are naturally more capable of handling the ups and downs, the surprises, the frustrations. While they are buoyant, others seem to falter or sink. So is there a solution? I believe there is! Research has shown that those who are emotionally competent are 10 times more likely to succeed than someone with high IQ alone. And the good news is that emotional competence can be developed and enhanced through gaining a greater understanding of how our minds process events, by monitoring personal experiences, and maintaining a conscious effort to build this competence.

Most organizations haven't, however, been very good at focusing on building emotional competence. There was a Harvard study that examined why people left sales careers. It was determined that 0% left because of product knowledge, 4% left because of lack of sales skills, 10% couldn't identify their reasons and 86% left because of emotional issues. Yet most training in the first years of someone's career is focused on

89

technical or analytical skills. Likewise, when people fail in leadership roles it is rarely because they lack technical or intellectual competence. Emotional Competence can be a leader's Achilles heel or it can be their greatest strength.

Emotional Competence Definition

Daniel Goleman was one of the first and is one of the most renowned leaders in developing the concept of Emotional Competence. He defines it as: *"A learned capability based on emotional intelligence that results in outstanding performance at work. Our emotional intelligence determines our potential for learning the practical skills based on the five elements: self awareness, motivation, self-regulation, empathy, and adeptness in relationships."* Let's take a look at each of these elements and see how we can build and develop them personally. The first three elements are related to Personal Competence and the last two elements are related to Social Competence.

PERSONAL COMPETANCE

Self Awareness

Self awareness is one of the most important elements to focus on when developing your emotional competence. We all have belief systems and values. Some of these have come from conscious decisions and some have come from stored emotional memories. It is crucial to become cognizant of what they are and to examine them to see if they are consistent with who you are and what you want to be.

These belief systems and values link quickly to emotions/feelings and those link to what you think, say, and do. There are many patterns of thought, emotions, and behaviors. Becoming aware of them is crucial if you want to reframe your thoughts and choose behaviors that are aligned with your goals and who you want to be. Also look for ways to become more aware of events that are "trigger events" for you. In other words, ask yourself what kinds of situations trigger certain emotions in you? What is your self talk and how do you respond? Is it in alignment with your values and what you want?

Realize that different people will have different feelings and thoughts for the very same event. Being self aware means being able to identify what you are feeling when it happens. As an example, let's say your monthly performance is below your goal and your leader is gruff with you. Are you feeling concerned, perplexed, frustrated, dismissive, ashamed, angry or justified? Being aware of your feelings will help you to manage your thoughts/self-talk and choose appropriate behaviors.

Another element of self awareness is an accurate assessment of one's strengths and a strong sense of self-worth or high self-esteem. I am sure that there are times when you wish you were someone else…that you had someone else's looks, talent, luck, etc. A bishop preaching to a congregation one Sunday asked everyone who had thoughts like that to raise their hand. Almost every hand in the church went up. He shook his head sadly and said, "When are you people going to get over it? The reason you are you is because everyone else is taken! You are all you have and it is wonderful!" It is easy to be critical and self judging but we need to spend more time recognizing our strengths and gifts.

Self Regulation
The self-talk that occurs after a triggering event can easily control your responses to an event and can contribute to your overall well being. Self-talk is our thoughts …the way you talk to yourself. Some estimates say that we have over 65,000

thoughts a day and that approximately 75% of those are negative, self critical or judgmental. Depressing as this sounds, there is something that you can do about it by managing your thoughts and breaking the cycle of negative self-talk.

A few years ago I had a direct report who was extraordinarily, emotionally competent. Every time we encountered a major problem or issue, he would immediately say, "Another opportunity to excel!" At first it used to irritate me and then I realized that he was taking a negative situation, breaking the cycle and redirecting the energy in a positive way.

You can manage your self-talk. You can break a cycle of negative self-talk going on in your mind. Self-talk leads to actions that can either enable you to succeed or to block your goals. You may or may not believe what someone else says about you, but you always believe what you say to yourself. Think about the power of your self-talk. Self-talk is a major determinant of success and you can choose to control it!

Motivation
The other day I was going fishing and went to a bait store. On the wall there was this beautiful poster of someone fishing in a boat at sunset.

The poster read as follows:
12 hours
6,197 casts
2 follows
1 strike
Damn, I hope it is this good again tomorrow!

Now that is motivation! Obviously, the "catch" wasn't the only thing that motivated this person. The journey was important too.

Emotionally competent people have an achievement drive, a commitment to their goals, initiative, and optimism. Are you in alignment? To build your emotional competence, you need to frequently assess where you are. Often people will realize that they are committed to an organization, a role, or certain goals but that their behaviors don't reflect that. They are out of alignment. That signals a huge opportunity to realign.

SOCIAL COMPETENCE

Empathy

Emotionally competent individuals sense others' feelings and take an active interest in their concerns. They look for ways to develop others and bolster their abilities. They can anticipate, recognize and meet others' needs. They aren't hesitant to cultivate opportunities and develop people who aren't like themselves. How many times have you seen managers trying to hire people that are clones of themselves? Think of the possibilities they are missing because of this limited view of the world. Last, but not least, someone with empathy knows how to read a group's emotional currents and power relationships. This doesn't just happen for most people; you need to make a concerted effort to pay attention to the dynamics.

Social Skills

This set of skills includes broad categories such as the ability to lead by inspiring and guiding, the ability to influence and implement tactics for persuasion. It also includes communication skills both in listening and in sending messages. An emotionally competent leader is not conflict adverse. They know how to address and manage conflict effectively. They also know how to create the dynamics for teaming and pursuing collective goals. They often do this through building relationships with people and working with them toward shared goals.

This last set of skills includes such a broad range of skills that doing a self assessment and getting feedback from others would be helpful in determining where you need to focus to improve your emotional competence.

Tips To Build and Enhance Your Emotional Competence

- Be aware of your self-talk and the feelings that generated it. If the self-talk is negative, break the cycle and create empowering self-talk.

- Use feelings and thoughts to help you make behavior choices. Try asking yourself these questions and then look at options for reframing and choosing the best behaviors. *How will I feel if I do this? How will I feel if I don't do this? How will I feel if I improve on the current status? What is an emotionally competent response to this and how do I get there?*

- Take personal responsibility for your feelings...e.g. *I feel frustrated vs. You make me feel frustrated.*

- Try to always label your feelings rather than labeling people or situations...e.g. *I am feeling very impatient and disappointed in this report vs. This report is ridiculous and you are a buffoon!*

- In most situations you can turn feeling angry into feeling energized. A favorite phrase of mine is, *"So what, now*

94

what?" Let's move on and do something about an issue instead of wallowing in it. Practice getting positive value from negative emotions.

- As much as possible, try to fill your world with emotionally competent people. Choosing to be around those with high emotional competence will naturally increase your own emotional competence!

- Put emotional competence on your radar screen. This is a muscle that can be developed; so get a plan, and monitor your experiences through conscious efforts and positive self-talk. This will have enormous impacts on your career, on your relationships, and your overall success.

It is time to get on the brain train and choose the right track! By being self-aware, managing your self-talk and thoughts, and choosing appropriate behaviors/actions you will continually enhance your emotional competence. All the data says that this leads to great achievements, success, and happiness. Sounds like a great destination!

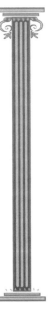

Chet Holmes has worked with over 60 of the Fortune 500 companies as America's top marketing executive, trainer, and strategic consultant. Chet is the author of the best selling book, <u>The Ultimate Sales Machine</u> (the #1 business book on Amazon, #1 sales and marketing book on Amazon, and also on the New York Times best seller list). Chet has identified and developed the 12 core competencies that are proven to provide the main structure of truly great companies and he has developed more than fifty proprietary methods to implement them. To learn more about how to double the sales of your company, go to:

www.howtodoublesales.com.

Chapter 8

The Ultimate Method for Developing Master-Level Salespeople

Chet Holmes

If you are interested in developing salespeople with master-level skills, this chapter will supply you with a method that will absolutely, positively help you accomplish this.

It is not necessarily the content of the following Seven Steps to Every Sale that will make this article revolutionary. These seven steps to every sale are fairly universal. There is, however, a principle that is essential for success with the seven steps.

No skill is gained by mere intellectual agreement

There is a missing ingredient to almost every sales training program, and it's not information. In fact, the "better" (based upon popularity) sales training programs usually have more information, better information, and even more advanced ideas and concepts. I've attended trainings on neuro-linguistic programming, for example, and been quite impressed with the idea of it, but have come away with no acquired skill.

Herein lays the problem with most sales training programs: You do not gain skill by intellectual agreement. For example, you might be very capable of understanding the principle behind a judo flip, but to be able to do it, you have to practice. To do it perfectly every time, you have to practice it continually.

If you've ever been part of a highly trained team, you know the sense of confidence that translates into success. The secret to building an excellent sales force (or team of any kind) is in repeating core training on basic sales skills again and again.

The Levels of Learning

The lowest level of learning is memorization. It is easy to memorize the seven steps to every sale, but that does not mean that you can apply them. However, it is an excellent starting point.

The highest level of learning is known as synthesis. This means that you have learned the material so well that you can synthesize it into your own style and method of doing things. Synthesis requires a lot of repetition and practice.

To achieve synthesis in your sales team, begin by having them commit the seven steps to memory, then set about polishing each skill area until your people are masters of each.

The Seven Steps to Every Sale

• **Establish rapport**. You will find that you close a much higher percentage of sales if you have good, solid rapport with your client. The ultimate definition of rapport is: they like you, they trust you, and they respect you. Respect and trust lead to influence. Influence leads to control over your market or the buying situation at hand. Work with your staff to design standards for establishing rapport.

• **Qualify the buyer (find the need)**. To reset a customer's buying criteria in favor of your product or service, you must begin by gaining a complete understanding of his or her current buying criteria. Develop the six to ten questions that you would like to know about every prospect before you begin to present your product or service. Drill these questions into your salespeople until they can recite them by heart.

• **Build value.** After you have assessed your customers buying criteria, you must begin to build value around your product or service. Make a presentation at this point in the sales process. The presentation should be targeted to the buyer, not to your product or service.

• **Create desire.** Be clear on this important point: your buyer will be a lot more motivated if his or her current situation becomes unacceptable. To create desire, you must motivate your buyer using a combination of problems and solutions, even if you are the one pointing out the problems that they haven't really considered. For example, one company that sold information services to accountants showed the accountants how much new tax information (statutes, regulations, tax law, tax cases, etc.) they have to know each year. This information made the accountants feel overwhelmed and predisposed to purchasing anything that would help them survive the tax-information plight. The company actually helped create the plight by introducing the accountants to the very real market statistics that existed but no one else was showing them. It was very, very powerful.

• **Overcome objections.** A talented salesperson does such a good job on finding the need that objections are covered earlier in the sales process. A top salesperson will qualify the buyer's buying criteria right down to his or her toes, before they even begin to sell. However, an objection can still surface when it is time to close the sale (see below). If you remember that "an objection is an opportunity to close," you will always be happy to hear one. For example:

a)   The client states an objection: "I'd love to buy it, but I just can't afford it right now."

b) Agree that the objection is valid. The client will drop his or her guard, "If you can't afford it, you can't afford it (meaningful pause). But let me ask you a question: is money the only thing standing between you and the purchase of this product?" At this point, if there are more objections, they will surface. If not, the client will say, "No, if I could afford it, I'd buy it." You have just moved a huge step closer to closing the sale.

c) Lock down the sale: you say, "So, if I can find a way for you to afford this product, you will buy it?" If the client says yes, you have just closed the sale. You will now need to be more creative in the financing of the product or service or help create more desire, so the prospect will pay the extra money to buy the product or service.

Getting   commitment   is   key   to   closing   the   sale.

• Close the sale—In truth, the best salespeople I have witnessed do not "close", they "bring the sale to a logical conclusion." They have helped set up such a logical buying criteria that the prospect and the salesperson walk to the close together. That being said, it should also be stated that most people need help making decisions.

This article cannot cover all the aspects of closing a sale, but it can cover the oldest close of all: assuming the sale. Do this by asking a question like, "Who do we send the bill to?" or "How did you want to pay for this?"

• Follow up — Last but not least, be prepared for The Cool-Off Factor. Because enthusiasm and rapport are extremely influential in the sales process, a salesperson must know that a prospect is going to "cool off" after the salesperson leaves the room.

How do you avoid this? Follow up strongly after the sale! The fax machine was the greatest invention for a salesperson. A good follow-up letter faxed hours after the sale, or the next day at the latest, can go a long way toward avoiding the cool-off factor.

Summary

These seven steps are core sales skills and procedures. Just as basketball coaches must constantly train their players on lay-up shots and blocking, sales managers must constantly train their players on polishing every angle of the Seven Steps to Every Sale.

Smart companies build tools, policies, and procedures that support these seven steps. The more standards you set, the higher the performance you can expect from every level of talent.

Go forth and master The Seven Steps to Every Sale. Only constant practice and repetition will create master-level salespeople.

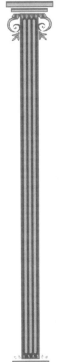

Dr. Robert Irwin is the founder of Sport of Mind, Inc.—a company committed to helping people reach their optimal state. With 12 years of clinical and sports psychology experience, Dr. Irwin created a secure and safe environment wherein people could discover and embrace their own possibilities. Initially Sport of Mind was established for the sole purpose of enhancing athletes' performance. When Dr. Irwin was presented with the opportunity to use his methodology for improving people's personal and professional lives, he found their results to be equivalent to that of his athletic clients. Now Sport of Mind offers the same proven success formula that has helped athletes to anyone who wants to tap into their inner source of power to improve their game—personal, professional or sports.

For suggested reading, visit my website at www.sportofmind.com. You can reach me at 619-884-3488 or email: drrob@sportofmind.com

Chapter Nine

New Pathways for Success

Dr. Robert Irwin

Everything, everything, EVERYTHING—your job, your spouse, the house you live in, the town you call home, and the clothes, cars, and friends you have—everything is based on your beliefs.

In this chapter, I will prove to you the truth of this statement— why this is true and how coaching helps you realize and reprogram your faulty belief systems into success-producing beliefs.

Ninety-percent of what we now know about the brain has been discovered in the last ten years. Scientists like Bruce Lipton, Louis Cozolino and Richard Restak are changing the collective wisdom in the field of neuroscience. We now have electron microscopes that can photograph an image that is the size of 1/100,000 of a human hair. We have learned that the brain is not limited to a fixed number of cells, but continues to grow. This is called *brain plasticity* or *neuroplasticity*. The brain grows new pathways and connections for as long as we continue to think. Those new pathways and their connections that send information automatically are the hardware of what we call *beliefs*. We now know that brain plasticity means that we can create new beliefs.

All of us have experienced how long will-power lasts, right?— until January 7th. Which is about the time you give up on that

New Year's resolution. That is because the nonconscious brain is overpowering the conscious brain. We have only recently learned about the nonconscious brain; it is 800 times faster and 5/6th bigger than the conscious brain. It remembers everything perfectly. This is like comparing the launch of the space shuttle to the launch of a paper airplane. The nonconscious brain never sleeps, never rests, never wanders—never stops working to produce the results that our beliefs expect. Its job is to solve the problems of our current predominant thoughts.

So how do we create our beliefs? Three ways; our conscious brain can willfully program them, our environment can program them, or a traumatic event can shape them.

The first way to create new beliefs is to willfully program them using the conscious brain. We generally create beliefs to solve an immediate problem or get through a certain era. And, we generally get the results we want. However, some beliefs are time-sensitive and they don't work as well when we keep going back to them. Like Johnny, who had a belief in grade school that he had to be #1 at everything or his dad wouldn't approve of him. It took hard work and dedication to be #1. So what did Johnny do? He said, "No" to high school parties and dances, and he buckled down. That belief worked in achieving his goal because he got strait A's and was the student body president of his high school. That belief was effective at the time, however, when he got older, he realized that being #1 was causing problems because he was so serious about being #1 that he was never home for his family. He needed to have a belief that his wife and family would love him even if he were not #1. As an adult, Johnny had to reprogram his brain to make a new belief. His new belief is, "I can win in my life and have fun doing it." He simply retrained his brain through repetition and association and created the environment around him to support this new belief and, lo and behold, he is much happier now.

The second way we shape our beliefs is environmental. Our nonconscious brain can pick up millions of bits of information every second that the conscious brain can't. If we are surrounded by upbeat, positive people, we are going to adopt their attitudes and beliefs. Likewise, if we are surrounded by people with negativity and low self-image, we will adopt those beliefs. So ask yourself, "What type of people do I currently surround myself with?"

Or the third way is waiting for some type of trauma in our lives, like cancer, a car accident, or death in the family, to drastically change our beliefs. We will have to wait and see what beliefs are changed. They may not be the beliefs that we want or need to change. Are you willing take that chance?

With this new information about the brain and the high-powered cameras available, we can take a picture of the brain thinking an old belief, reprogram it with affirmations, and take a picture afterwards to *see* the difference—the new growth, new pathways are the new beliefs. If we do this reprogramming long enough, that belief becomes the dominant system that drives the results we want automatically.

We now know our conscious brain can train our nonconscious brain through our "willful" thoughts, and these thoughts program deeper and deeper into our nonconscious brain through repetition, association and emotion. These programmed thoughts form intricate thought-patterns which, as we know now, are our beliefs.

105

Neurologists say we have between 65,000 and 166,000 thoughts per day. Ninety-five percent of those thoughts are the same thoughts we had yesterday. We are very much creatures of habit—robotic—which is a good thing. Otherwise we would have to learn to walk and brush our teeth each new day. Ninety-five percent of our functions occur at the auto-pilot level and the nonconscious brain is running the program. Do you remember having to think about how to eat your breakfast, brush your teeth or drive to work? Now you know why it is so hard to remember what you had for breakfast just yesterday, because you were in auto-pilot mode. That is why athletes practice the same skills over and over. They want to make sure that they are performing their duties on the field automatically. They don't want to stop and think about how to kick a field goal or catch a pass. People perform best when it's automatic.

We know that the majority of decision making and thought processes occur automatically in the nonconscious brain. The more we focus our thoughts on any given subject, could be a goal or a solution to a problem, the nonconscious brain starts to create solutions and instructions to make those thoughts reality. Its purpose is to solve the problems or create associations that are taking place in the conscious brain. If my predominant thoughts are, "Oh, I am not good enough," my brain is going to make sure that I am not good enough.

This is where what I call the "Belief Matrix" becomes useful. We know that beliefs drive our attitudes. Attitudes drive emotions. Emotions drive actions. Actions create our reality, or results. A diagram of that looks like this:

Beliefs → Attitudes→ Feelings → Actions → Results.
To learn what our beliefs are, we can simply look at our results. This Belief Matrix works in both directions. We know that 95%

of our thoughts are the same thoughts we had yesterday, which means that 95% of what we do is automatic and repetitious. Ninety-five percent of the time the chain of events in the matrix will be happening automatically.

As a coach it is difficult to get to the root of results, happy or unhappy. There is not a coaching model that gets to the truth of core beliefs like my Belief Matrix process.

For example, I worked with a woman named Lisa, who was perpetually in debt. It caused a tremendous amount of stress and anxiety in her life and it kept her from seeing many options available to her. Let's examine her belief system in reverse order:

Result → Debt
Action → Overspending and impulsive shopping
Feeling → Emptiness
Attitude → Nobody likes me
Belief → I'm not good enough

So far, this Belief Matrix has been 100% accurate on discovering faulty beliefs. (My clients get their desired results because, once we uncover the belief system that needs to change, we can start proactively programming healthy beliefs. This process is quite difficult to do alone. It is like a doctor trying to do surgery on a loved one; their emotions get in the way and cloud their thinking. So please seek the guidance of an experienced and qualified coach.

To use the Belief Matrix to create a powerful belief that will automatically lead to positive results, we simply start with the results we want. Let's look at Lisa's new Belief Matrix regarding her finances:

107

Result → Money in the bank (savings)

Action → Budgeting (spend wisely)

Feeling → Happy, peaceful, loving (care about myself)

Attitude → Thankful (grateful for what I have)

Belief → I am loved and I am good enough

The predominant, former belief of "I am not good enough" caused the nonconscious brain to produce the results that were automatically proving that belief to be true. Remember, the nonconscious brain is robotic and it will naturally respond to your predominant thoughts. Those beliefs such as "I'm not worth it," means, 95% of the time what we get are worthless results. If we think "I'm loved" guess what kind of results we get? Life-affirming results 95% of the time!

To summarize, I told you about the new discoveries that show that our brains are capable of growing and learning until the day we die. This discovery is called "brain plasticity." We make our brains grow with new, conscious thoughts. Generally, beliefs are created because they were pertinent at the time and solved a problem.

To proactively create beliefs to get the results we want, we need to write new software for the hardrive—our nonconscious brain—to run. We can use our 5% conscious brain to train the 95%, ever-powerful, nonconscious brain.

The key to effective coaching is knowing "the why and the how," like the nutritionist to food and dieting, or the trainer to knowing how the body operates—the coach needs to know how thoughts create your reality.

Now, let's go make the right change!

**The wisest Coaches
will educate their Players
not to accept reasons or excuses
in place of results.**

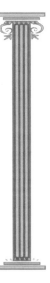

Brian Tracy is the most listened to audio author on personal and business success in the world, today. He is the author/narrator of countless best-selling audio learning programs and the author of 16 books. All rights reserved worldwide.

Contact Brian Tracy at: Brian Tracy International, 462 Stevens Ave., Suite 202, Solana Beach, CA 92075
Phone: (858) 481-2977
www.BrianTracy.com

Copyright © 2006

Chapter 10

Thinking Like A Winner

Brian Tracy

After studying the research done in cognitive psychology over the last 25 years, I've come to a simple conclusion: The degree to which you feel in control of your life will largely determine your level of mental well-being, your peace of mind, your happiness and the quality of your interactions with people. Cognitive psychologists call this a "sense of control." It is the foundation of happiness and high achievement. And the only thing in the world over which you have complete control is the content of your conscious mind. If you decide to exert that control and keep your mind on what you want, even when you are surrounded by difficult circumstances, your future potential will be unlimited.

Your aim should be to work on yourself and your thinking until you reach the point where you absolutely, positively believe yourself to be a total winner in anything you sincerely want to accomplish. When you reach the point where you feel unshakable confidence in yourself and your abilities, nothing will be able to stop you. And this state of self-confidence comes from, first, understanding the functioning of your remarkable mind and, second, practicing the techniques of mental fitness over and over, until you become a completely optimistic, cheerful and positive person.

Italian psychologist Dr. Roberto Assagioli left us two

113

remarkable pieces of writing, <u>Psychosynthesis</u> and <u>The Act of Will</u>. In those books, Assagioli brought his remarkable intelligence to bear on the entire subject of human potential and human happiness. He studied the mind and personality for his entire lifetime, and he came up with several ideas that are profoundly simple and powerfully effective in helping you and me to lead happier, more satisfying lives. In The Act of Will, he laid out a series of psychological principles, or laws, that can be very helpful to you in understanding the way your mind works and how you can take control of it.

The third of Assagioli's laws is that images or pictures, either from within or from the outside, will trigger thoughts and feelings consistent with them. In turn, those thoughts and feelings will trigger behaviors that lead to the realization of the pictures. For example, when you become absolutely convinced that you are a total winner and you are meant to be a complete success in anything that you really want to do, every picture or image that you see that somehow represents winning to you will trigger thoughts of what you could do to achieve that same state. The picture will also trigger the feeling of excitement that will motivate you to take action.

A friend of mine who was a sales manager had a simple technique to make new salespeople successful, and it worked in more than 90 percent of cases. When he hired a salesperson, he would take that person to a nearby Cadillac dealership and force the person to trade in his current car on a new Cadillac. The payments on the Cadillac would be substantially more than the new salesperson had ever imagined paying, and he would strongly resist getting into the commitment. However, the sales manager would insist until, finally, the salesperson bought the new Cadillac and drove it home.

No matter how unsure or insecure the salesperson felt, when his spouse and friends saw the new Cadillac and he experienced the pleasure of driving it down the street, he began to think about himself and to see himself as a big success selling his product. And in almost all cases, it turned out to be true. Those salespeople went on to become great successes in their field.

Take every opportunity you can to surround yourself with images of what success means to you: Get brochures on new cars; get magazines containing pictures of beautiful homes, beautiful clothes and other things that you could obtain as a result of achieving the success that you are aiming for. Each time you see or visualize those images, you trigger the thoughts, feelings and actions that make them materialize in your life.

Assagioli's fourth law is that thoughts, feelings and images trigger the words and actions consistent with them. This is another way of saying that your inner impressions will motivate you to pursue the outer activities that will move you toward the achievement of your goals.

Assagioli's fifth law is that your actions will trigger thoughts, emotions and images consistent with them. That has been referred to as the Law of Reversibility. It is one of the most important success principles ever discovered.

Simply, that law says that you are more likely to act yourself into feeling than you are to feel yourself into acting. On many days, you wake up feeling not as positive and optimistic as you would like. However, if you act as if you already have the feeling that you desire, the action itself will trigger the feelings and the thoughts and mental pictures consistent with them.

In her book Wake Up and Live, Dorothea Brande said that the most important success secret she ever discovered was this: "Act as if it were impossible to fail, and it shall be."

In the book, she goes on to explain that you need to be very clear about the success that you desire, and then simply act as if you already had it. Act as if your success were inevitable. Act as if your achievement were guaranteed. Act as if there were no possibility of failure.

The wonderful thing is this: You can control your actions easier than you can control your feelings. If you choose to exert control over your actions, those actions will have a "back flow" effect and trigger the feelings, thoughts and images that are consistent with those of the person you want to be, of the person who lives the life you want to live. There is a principle called the Law of Expression, which says that whatever is expressed is impressed. This means that whatever you say, whatever you express to another in your conversation, is impressed into your subconscious mind.

The reverse of this law is that whatever is impressed will, in turn, be expressed. It will come out. Your conversation reveals an enormous amount about you, the kind of person you are and the things that you believe about yourself and others.

In identifying those laws, one of the most important facts I discovered is that your brain is a multi-sensory, multi-stimulated, extremely complex, interactive organ. Everything that you think, imagine, say, do or feel triggers everything else, like a chain reaction, or like a series of electrical impulses going out in all directions and turning on lights everywhere.

Let's say that you are driving down the street, listening to the radio and thinking about a variety of things. Suddenly, you hear a song that you associate with an old romance that you had many years before. Instantaneously, your brain reacts and re-creates all the sensations that were present when you were with that person a long time ago. You instantly get a mental picture of the person. You see and remember where you were and what you were doing when the song was playing back then. You feel the emotion that you experienced at that time. You recall what was going on around you-the sounds, the season, the lights, the people and the activities. You temporarily forget whatever you were thinking about and are transported, in a split second, back across the years. Sometimes, the emotion that you recall is so intense that it brings you close to tears or fills you with happiness.

That is the way your mind works. By understanding that, you can make your mind work for you as a powerful engine of growth and development. You can consciously surround yourself with a series of sensory inputs that bombard you with messages and cause you to think and feel like a total winner.

Thinking like a winner is the first step to living like a winner. You do become what you think about most of the time. You are not what you think you are; but what you think, you are. In fact, you are what you most intensely believe. And if you think and act like a winner, keeping your mind positive and optimistic, you will be a winner.

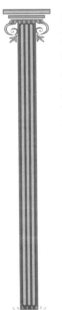

Scott Taylor is the Founder and CEO of TaylorMade Marketing, LLC a Los Angeles based creative agency formed in 1996 and focused on search engine optimization, copy and design for business collateral materials, creation and maintenance of ecommerce web sites and promotional campaigns online and in print.

Scott is also the President of FastPath Coaching (A TaylorMade Marketing Company) providing FastPath Action Plans to small business owners and sales professionals via coaching, seminars, and workshops year round. Scott can be reached at FastPath Coaching by calling 818-344-6800, email at scott@fastpathcoaching.com and online at www.fastpathcoaching.com

Chapter 11

Imagine • Create • Deliver
A Foundation of Achievement

Scott Taylor

I am here to tell you, without a shadow of a doubt, that anyone with a strong will, and a healthy desire to do so, can be an absolute winner in the sales game--and we are all in the sales game. We sell ideas to each other, and we are selling all day long. I don't care what your business is, you are already selling, you are using established habits and have been your whole life.

Those of us who make our income by selling products and services are just slightly more focused on the study, the art, and the science of the craft.

All you really need is the ability to understand, or comprehend a few step-by-step instructions to launch a brilliant earning potential. Once you have the initial instructions, you must get yourself to take specific action for a sustained period, and I don't know how long it will take you. I have seen complete amateurs get things swinging in a few days, and others take a few months. As many have shared--we tend to get out of life what we put into it, and I know that has been true for me, and the companies I have created.

I like to simplify complex concepts whenever possible. In doing this type of study, attempting to identify how and what makes things work, I realized that as we create our lives, we give the

119

meaning to what shows up through our memories, thoughts, our beliefs, and finally by the formation of our habits. The best news is that you can use the same process with a conscious focus to create better habits. My suggestion is to make the   best effort possible to imagine, create and deliver the income-producing habits you want!

Since we know that we are habitual creatures, we know how habits are created. We have a few keys to establishing the life of our dreams. It's helpful to understand that our thoughts create our beliefs. Beliefs are simply thoughts we keep thinking. We learn these thoughts from those we love and respect, and although they mean well, they may not have the correct information. If you ever find yourself stuck, frustrated, and unable to break through to more successful results, it's likely connected to your habits.

Seek out and find the best possible answers, ideas, books, mentors and/or partners if necessary and never stop searching until you are satisfied.

Beliefs and habits, to a large degree, control your comfort zones, your level of fear, and up to 96% of what you will or will-not do in your current state of mind. You will have to bust out of the habits, and the comfort zones that are holding you back.

This is an inside issue. Allow your nature to work for you instead of against you. There is a great saying in the coaching community, "If you can't, you must!" This is all about busting through your fears. Fear is the culprit, and it's an imagined stimulus, so consider using the power of your imagination for your goals as well. The simplest form I know of, and a good way to begin is to use the process I call "Imagine • Create • Deliver™!"

Imagine: Seek clarity. Clarity is very important. Set your intention and imagine that you already have what you want, as you want it, and feel the excitement, the thrill, and the joy of having it as often and as creatively as you can. Use as many of your sensory factors as possible in doing this.

Create: Map out how others have done it. Get help through books, audio programs, making phone calls to anyone you can find that may have answers to your questions regarding the objective. You must take serious levels of ACTION daily, or as often as you can to ensure that the learning curve, the implementation, and ongoing creation process is unfolding to make it happen. Expect it and act on it often!

Deliver: Set a timeline to baby-step your way to deliver the results you need. The timeline serves to measure your progress, it will also provide urgency, and connect you to your commitments, and perhaps, most important to this lesson, committing to your timeline over the course of one, two and three months (or whatever it takes) you will establish the all important habits of a winner.

As a sales and marketing coach, I have helped more people reach and exceed quotas and personal financial goals by challenging their thoughts, beliefs, and ultimately their habits. This is all about your mindset for the purpose of establishing winning habits! When you do this well, your career and your life can begin to flow. You'll wonder how you didn't think of this long ago!

A good start for a healthy mindset in sales is the knowledge and belief that, "Selling is a process, not an event!" In breaking down what happens in most sales cycles, you will likely find a series of small easy agreements prior to the more serious qualifying stage.

In many circles it is called trail closing, small talk, or establishing rapport. Others simply begin doing this in the greeting stage. This can show up as a few simple, obvious questions, humorous comments, or statements that the sales person will ask or share, and with which anyone with good common sense would smile and agree, i.e. "I'll assume you want the best deal possible today, is that right?"

The reason humor, and creative trail-closing are so effective is that they help us to establish a warm human connection when done well. The point is to simply help the prospect loosen up, feel comfortable with us, and talk more openly. It's very difficult to sell the right solution unless we can bring down the walls of fear and fear is found on both sides of the wall! It's a small easy point for sure, but without it, or something like it, you run the risk of killing a sale because most people agree that they need to like you first. The final point here is that early smiles and agreements on smaller points help the salesperson lead the prospect through the process in a structured order which keeps the flow of the decisions moving forward towards the final resolve.

Your success is impacted by how you communicate, approach your projects, and function in a social environment. It is also impacted by your past experiences, as well as your strengths and your nature. There are many paths to a worthy goal, and your task is to find your own. Your best path is often not going to be the same as for others. In fact most really successful people in all fields clearly state again and again, that showing up in their own unique way, and letting their natural talents shine and develop is exactly why they are so successful.

This is also why they are so happy. Wherever it's appropriate, I like to encourage my clients and students to let their natural genius, and their unique personality be nurtured, developed, and honored in their life's work. Do this and you can truly thrive. But also for those of you who are creating your own product or service, use common sense and make sure that the market wants what you're selling. The feedback from a few early tests will indicate some of the corrections you will need to make. Likewise, a good mastermind session with some smart, successful friends, associates or those you trust is worth its weight in gold. Use it as a reality check to determine the true potential of the systems you will be using.

I say it that way because in many occupations, or new positions you need to first learn and test things the way the company, or the trainer, or mentor is teaching them. Then you can change things and put our own twist on them after you learn the basic skills, or processes as taught first. That's important.

It is said often, and by many who know, that: "Sales is the highest paid hard work you will ever find on the planet, and it's also the lowest paid, easy work."

So, consider that, as you 'sharpen your axe'. You can have it all; the cars, the homes, the travel, the creature comforts and all the details of your greatest wants and wishes - if you will make the deals happen. One of my mentors likes to say that your raise in pay will become "effective" the very second that you are!

So let's jump into the sales lessons I have prepared for you:
I like to start with Mindset. Mindset is about how we approach the task at hand. I believe to my core that words are symbols of mindset. The words you choose to use in your thoughts and

verbal communications will provide power to your cause, or they will block you.

As you evolve in your career, I believe that your words need to evolve to shape your mindset, to help you create the inner game that provides the power and skills you need to become as effective as you want to be.

Specifically, I am talking about the basic words we use in sales training that will trip up, rip up, and hick-up your chances at making the launch you want.

"Cold call" is one of those words. A big one! What matters most is the meaning you give it. Your brain will release the chemical to match how words and their meanings make you feel, and they will prolong this feeling, this emotion, that will either serve you, or create barriers to entry.

How does the thought of "cold calling" make you feel? Think about it with some serious intent. We all need to identify, or source new contacts, introduce ourselves, ask some questions to see if we are a good match, and if there is potential to move forward to qualify the prospect in some degree.

Do you feel good or not-so-good about making lots of cold calls? I think you'll find that for most people the experience of "cold calling" is a less-than-good feeling.

The point again is that words matter. How we think about things really, really matters! If you are going to create your own "FastPath" to success, to joy, to the life you really want, you need to consider your mindset. Your mindset will always be affected by your thoughts; your thoughts will always be affected by the words you choose to use. Once again, this may seem like a small point, but it's a foundation principle that is at the core of these new habits that will get you on autopilot to the success you seek by virtue of how your thoughts and beliefs help you, or hinder you from creating the winning habits.

This calls to Intention, which is another point of the mindset issue. If you are going to enhance your life, your powerful intention to do this work will provide the power to make your life more productive. You can often accomplish more of your desires with less agony and effort, by using intention. Often you can do this easily by first correcting any issues with your mindset. Got it? Say YES! That's what I'm taking about, words matter, thoughts matter. Make sense? I heard Jim Cathcart speak to this and he shared a very clear point about the power of our words and why we should focus on catching ourselves when we use a negative expression habitually. He simply asked: "Why would we poison the well before we drink?"

Another big word which will weaken, block, or hold you back a bit is the word *selling*. I personally love and respect the word - but I am very aware that many people think of selling as a negative word. If this includes you, I want you to change the word to one that empowers you, such as serving, or helping, or it could be consulting or coaching someone through an important decision they need to make. You are there to help them process the facts, consider the choices, and make the best decision possible. The point again, is to choose your thoughts, your words, and the meanings you give them so that you are "feeling" right. So much power comes from feelings.

A word of caution--I am not talking about semantics! These are real issues I am addressing. According to most people who get into sales, cold calling is perhaps the least desirable function of the job. I believe that is an established fact and a big issue.

125

I also believe that common sense will prove that our mindset makes this so. If we truly want to serve others, I know for myself that it just feels so much better to make new calls, when I have prepared, and rehearsed a great message into a great script. I know exactly what the essence of my message is, and I know exactly what I'm going to say. Further more, I have gone over every possible objection with my team (or mastermind group) to further ensure that I feel confident, and can even look forward to the chance to engage with my calls because I did my research. I am ready to share my findings with the people I believe will benefit the greatest and the work is so much more rewarding.

When you have this work behind you, and the facts are on your side, the level of integrity and honor is high. This is no longer an issue of fearing cold calls; you are an expert on this subject—a total professional—and your position helps people to solve problems and to reach their goals and objectives. You "get" to do this instead of the old way of thinking which was I "have" to do this to pay my bills. That's a mindset shift worth making!

Another big point is that you really need to go deeper to understand that this is why and how the champions stand out above the competition. You need to understand how your products and services help people. And you need to gain clarity on everything you do to enhance this. Then you can get in the habit of keeping these benefits front and center as you begin. The purpose is to help keep your mindset positive and motivated as you gain experience. Once you have several months behind you, using this framework, you will likely rise to the pro levels and produce the results of a professional sales executive. This is a total win-win for everyone!

When this work is done right, you will already know 95% of the objections, as well as the best possible replies to help your clients understand how important your product or service is to their expressed objectives, desires or needs.

The professional sales executive is studied, sharp, skillful, trustworthy, consultative, and enjoys helping people make smart decisions to enhance their lives in all relevant areas whenever possible. It all starts with a clear idea of what you want, and then you identify and commit to an action plan to get it in gear. You try out the ideas, you begin testing early and often, correcting as you go where ever needed. You establish organized systems that quickly become habits, which you now know, are key to making it all happen. I don't recall who said it, but it's this: "Think of S.Y.S.T.E.M. as **S**ave **Y**our **S**elf **T**ime, **E**nergy, and **M**oney!" It is so true.

Systems become habits that you will do on an automatic response within a short time. So, your success becomes tied to your habits! Your level of required effort will decrease as the habits are established. Life becomes so much better as this stage.

Always ask for the help you need as you are working to create the new habits. You'll find endless answers and creative suggestions, which in turn create unlimited potential by reading the best-selling books and staying committed to making it happen, and finally you deliver! Once you hit the mark or make it to your expressed goal(s), you must up level your goals and continue the natural growth and evolution that is your nature! Enjoy!

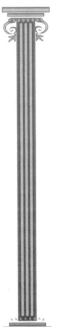

Don Boyer, creator of the best-selling The Power of Mentorship series, is an outstanding speaker and a proficient published author. His mission, passion and purpose are to help you reach your full potential. He is a proud father and grandfather and resides in Southern California with his wonderful wife, Melinda.

Contact Don by telephone at 562-789-1909 or by email to:

donboyer@realifeteaching.com or
don@donboyer.org

Visit his website at www.realifeteaching.com.

Copyright 2007 by Don Boyer/ Real Life Teaching Inc.

128

Chapter 12

The Hidden Secret to Achievement

Don Boyer

Do you realize that money is just a symbol for value? The money you *have* is your report card of what you *give*. Your bank account reflects your value account. If you watch the actions, mindset and habits of the average person or business that is struggling financially, you will find that they are more interested in making money than they are in producing value.

There is one thing that you cannot do, and that is you cannot deceive the business market. The business market only responds to releasing its funds to value. How do you create value in the marketplace, for your customer, family or humanity? I have found four powerful ways.

1. Dump the Scarcity Mindset

The scarcity mindset is the reason people live their lives and/or run their businesses based on making money and not on adding or creating value for people. Thus, every area of their lives, where they apply this method, financially and personally, is a struggle. They do this because of an internal belief (a paradigm) that there is not enough for everyone, and for them to have enough they must somehow win the battle and get yours.

Recently I met a very bright young man (in his twenties) with a family to support, who was making just enough to get by. I took him to lunch a couple of times and he really wanted me to mentor and help him. I gave him a small--one day--job working in my office and offered to pay him $500.00. The first thing he asked me was when I would pay him? Then he asked how long did he have to work? Then he wanted to know if lunch was included.

It was not that this young man was lazy, nor did he intend to come across like someone walking around in a fog, it was just that his mindset was that of being more interested in what he got verses in what he could give. Although he has great potential, this mindset will keep him locked in poverty, just getting by.

"The great tragedy of life is...
People can have so much but settle for so little".
                                        ---Don Boyer

I have a family member who also suffers from this scarcity mindset and, like the young man above, does not have two quarters to rub together from his paycheck.

He and I were eating out the other day, and his rudeness became intolerable. Upon getting his lunch he dove right in, without waiting for others to get their food, and began chewing with his mouth open. I slammed my fist on the table and said, "David (not his real name), how does it feel to be the only person on the planet?" He looked up at me and said, "I wish I were, that way I could have everything just for me". Very sad; sad that he lives like this and sad that millions of people operate and run their businesses and lives with this very mindset.

If you want to spot a winner, become aware of those you eat out with. A winner will pick up the check; a loser expects you to. On a good day, a loser may say, "I will get the tip" and then leave a dollar! You cannot possibly get ahead in life or financially with a scarcity mindset.

2. Be on a Mission

Ask yourself everyday, "How can I bring my customers, marketplace, friends, business and family more value? This is a foundational principle that we use to run our company and our lives. Does this mean you should give away your product or service? Sometimes. Let me give you an example. Our mission and purpose is to give people the opportunity to better their lives. One way that I do that is by giving away free Mentorship books and free Mentorship kits. But, my mission is to help people, not waste or throw away my money. So, when people go to my website www.DonBoyerAuthor.com to get their free book or Mentorship kit, I ask them to pay the small shipping and handling fee. If someone is not willing to pay the shipping charge to get a free book or kit that thousands have paid full price for, they are not the ones I can help.

When we first launched this offer, a friend said to me, "What a great marketing plan." I said, "I am not doing this as a marketing plan; I am doing this so that I can bring value to those who want to improve themselves, and I don't want to waste money on those who only want a free ride in life."

"The worst day in a man's life is when he expects something for nothing."
— *Thomas Jefferson*

There is a huge difference between giving value and wasting money. My view is you feed a jackass corn, not gold! Value should be given to those who deserve value (which is most people). Do you know those in your life who deserve gold and

131

those who deserve corn? Your ability to know the difference will be a key factor in your overall success.

3. Million Dollar Service

Create a plan to give people what I call "Million Dollar Service". Model it after the kind of service you receive from an exclusive hotel or high-end restaurant. Make a list of five things you can do for your customers that are above and beyond your call of duty. Small gestures can create a big impact. It is very important that you base these gestures on the foundation of value and of caring for people.

Do not use it as a means to dig deeper into their pockets, as a con job, but instead use it as a means to say "Thank You" and "I really appreciate your business." In other words, make it a true value that comes from the heart of service.

4. Develop the Trust Factor

People must trust you. This is one, if not the most important, factor that you must develop if you plan to have long-term success in your business, finances, relationships and life. This is a characteristic you cannot fake. People invest in my services because of one main factor; they trust me. Trust must be earned. Trust comes from being transparent and honest with people, by being a master of what you do, your product or service being the best on the market and by providing unparalleled value.

If you develop a reputation of untrustworthiness, plan on living like a vagabond in the business world. Being a person who cannot be trusted to keep your word or commitments, or conducts business in such a way that you always end up with the bigger share is a sure path to financial and business ruin. And think about this: if you cannot trust someone to return a phone call, do you think you can trust them to return value for your money?

The fastest path to cash is to understand that when you increase your value to the market place, you automatically increase your income and profits. Work on creating value, and the money will take care of itself.

And that is the "Hidden Secret to Achievement."

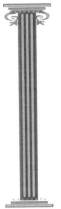

Jim Rohn is *America's Foremost Business Philosopher*.

To subscribe to the Free Jim Rohn Weekly E-Zine, visit www.jimrohn.com or send a blank email to subscribe@jimrohn.com.

Chapter 13

Preparation for Your Presentations

Jim Rohn
Adapted from the Jim Rohn Weekend Event –
Excelling in the New Millennium

Persistence in your presentations, this is one secret to success. After my first presentation, I got up and did it again. Even though I was scared to death, I did it again. And that second one wasn't too good, but guess what. I did it again, and I did it again. And I worked up my courage, and I did it again. I committed to it, and I did it again. And finally, it got to be a little bit easier. I got a little more acquainted with the art of presenting. So have something good to say in your presentations. Preparation for your presentations, this is another key aspect. Here are some words to help you in preparation.

To prepare to have something good to say, keep a keen interest in life and people. Don't let your senses go dull here. Guess what most people are trying to do – get THROUGH the day. Here is what I am asking this unusual audience to do – get FROM the day. Get from the day a clear picture of the drama of human life – some doing is right, some doing is wrong. Some gathering in; some throwing it away. Some building reputations; some letting it all slide.

Get from the day what is happening in politics. Read the newspapers. Read the magazines. Find out what's going on. Get from the periodicals. Get from what's happening. Get from your job. Get from your career. Get from the people around you. What is happening in the community? Get from all of that. The positive side, the negative side.

My parents used to say, "Attend everything." Some things are so costly; they might be out of reach for a while. Andrea Bocelli came to Beverly Hills. Guess what the tickets cost? $2500.00 for a two-hour performance. That is pretty good pay. So some things might be out of reach, but whatever you can go to, get to. Save up the money and go, so that you will be more aware of what is going on around you.

Keep up that interest in people. Why do they do what they do? How come things are happening today that didn't happen thirty years ago?

Now the next word is fascination. Be fascinated with life and people and drama that is live and in color every day. Cinemascope. Fascination goes a little bit beyond interest. Interested people want to know does it work. Fascinated people want to know how does it work.

Kids have this unique ability to learn several languages in a six, seven-year period, and the reason is because they are so fascinated. They are so interested. They are so curious. Kids have to know, and that is how the drama of their learning takes on such speed in a fairly short period of time is because of this unusual interest and fascination and curiosity. We're walking on ants, and kids are studying them. They say, "Don't walk on those ants. I'm studying them." How come an ant can carry

136

something bigger than they are? That is a good question. They must be unbelievably strong if they can carry something bigger than they are.

Here is something else I've learned. To be fascinated instead of frustrated. It is just a little trick to play. The next time you're tempted to be frustrated, see if you can't turn it into fascination. Instead of a frown, it puts a smile on your face. Now sometimes you look a little weird, but so be it. He says, "How can he smile?" I don't know. He must be somebody different.

Babe Ruth – Home Run King – back in those days of baseball used to strike out and come back to the bench smiling. They used to say, "Babe, you just struck out. How can you smile?" "I'm just that much closer to my next home run. Just stick around. It won't be long. One will be sailing over the fence." So find things fascinating instead of frustrating. Just try it. I've learned how to do it. Now make this note. It doesn't work every time. Nothing works every time, but every time you can get it to work, guess what? It will benefit your day. You'll get more from it. You'll be fascinated instead of frustrated.

Now I've also learned the ultimate. I'm fascinated by my own frustration. How come it doesn't take me long to loose it on occasion? It must be from my father's side. My mother was a gentle soul. Just find it all fascinating. I've talked to a lot of the Network Marketing companies over the years, and I give them that little clue. Somebody joins and you think they're going to stay forever, and they leave right away. You have to say, "Isn't that interesting?" And someone you thought would never make it, sure enough they become superstars. You have to say, "Isn't that interesting?" You say, "I thought they'd stay forever, they don't stay. Isn't that interesting. I didn't think they'd do anything, look what they're doing. Isn't that interesting?"

So that is a good phrase. Find it interesting. Find it fascinating. Wow, I never thought that would happen. I had another picture in mind. Wow! Was I ever wrong. And it's good sometimes to be wrong on the positive side. I didn't think it was going to work, and it worked. Say, "What if somebody doesn't look at your business opportunity?" Say, "What if they do?" It doesn't take much to turn the question around. Say, "What if they won't join after they look?" "What if they do? What if they join and stay." But I've got a better question, "What if they do stay?" "What if they quit after three months?" I have a better question, "What if they stay?"

So sometimes little tricks you can play to give yourself a different look because somebody could either stay or leave and wouldn't it be better to assume that they would stay and then if they leave say, "Isn't that interesting?" I have learned to do that with myself. "Wow! Look what I did. Isn't that interesting? Wow! I thought I was going to behave better. Wow! I lost it. Isn't that interesting? I thought for sure that wasn't going to bother me. Sure enough. I thought I had a handle on this. Looks like I've got some work to do." Find yourself fascinating and interesting as you journey through life. Give yourself a chance.

Now here is the next word that is very important if you want to be a good communicator, and that is sensitivity. Sensitive to someone's drama and trouble and difficulty. As you contemplate your own, now you can be sensitive to someone else. And there is no better way to be helpful than to do your best to try and understand. Here is the old phrase we've heard it, let's jot it down this time. "Learn to walk in someone's shoes

138

for a while. Try to understand where they are." How come they're in this dilemma? Maybe it's something I don't know. I don't understand. How come this person is losing his temper when he should keep it? Who knows what might have happened the last three weeks. I don't know. Let's give somebody room by trying to understand.

Be sensitive to someone lashing out and being difficult at the time. Hey! We can handle that. We don't have to retaliate and fight back. Can't we say, "Maybe there's a good reason this person behaves in this way." That is an easier way. Sensitivity. Trying to understand. Trying to comprehend the full drama of human experience. One of the greatest phrases in the Bible, "Blessed are the peacemakers." Guess what a peacemaker is? Someone that you hope is around when the conflict could be resolved. Someone who understands both sides and brings them together. Say, "I know you've got some animosity, but now that you've fought and that didn't settle it...couldn't we get together and reason this whole thing out?"

So in times of conflict, we look for a peacemaker. And the peacemaker has to understand both sides of the issue. Say, "I understand your dilemma, and I can see where you're coming from, and I can understand why you said what you said then you said what you said. But hey! Isn't there a better way? Couldn't we find a better way to settle it all?" And that is what we are looking for.

Parents have to learn to be peacemakers when there are two sides to an issue and maybe neither one is that far wrong. But to try to settle it, we have to understand both sides. We have to understand the feelings on both sides, and that kind of sensitivity gives us a wonderful opportunity to grow, so that we can communicate and our words will be meaningful. Then the test comes, and the drama comes and the time comes to step up and speak or to sit down and speak or to be quiet and speak or to be loud and speak. Whatever that might call for, we'll be prepared if we do have a genuine understanding. So preparation in all areas of life is so vital to your success. Don't be lazy in preparing; don't be lazy in laying the groundwork that will make all of the difference in how your life turns out.

"As to methods there may be a million and then some, but principles are few. The man who grasps principles can successfully select his own methods. The man who tries methods, ignoring principles, is sure to have trouble."

– Ralph Waldo Emerson

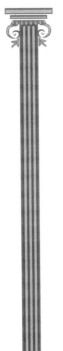

Debra J. Satterwhite, ABR and Spiritual Director has been working in the real estate field since 1976. Prior to joining her current real estate firm where she is a Member of the Top Ten and local Association of Realtors® Masters Club, she achieved membership in RE/MAX's 100% and Platinum Clubs. One of her unique abilities is "systems" consulting for real estate professionals.

Debra completed her Spiritual Direction training at the Spiritual Director's Institute, Burlingame, California and is a member of Spiritual Directors International. Her interest in relational health brings a unique spin to her real estate consulting and Spiritual Direction work. Debra can be reached at debras@nccn.net or telephone her at: (530) 271-3870.

142

Chapter 14

Define It! Build It! Own It!

Debra J. Satterwhite

No one on earth has your exact same personality, experiences and style. Whatever you choose to do in your life, no one can do it, say it, or be it quite like you. You are unique; one-of-a-kind. As am I.

When I think about the fact that every snowflake is different, I'm in awe. How can that be possible? Why would God bother? I think it is a reminder—remember the "big picture" calling of life. Simply put—to be YOU!

Share your gifts and talents in the unique, one-of-a-kind way only you can! And, do it with integrity, respect and love.

So, with that in mind, I humbly share with you my secrets of achievement. They are as follows: (1) Defining achievement for YOU, (2) Building strong personal foundations and (3) Owning your journey.

Defining Achievement for YOU

Webster Dictionary defines achievement as "something accomplished, as through great effort, skill, perseverance or courage." So, what do you want to achieve? Name it, claim it and don't apologize for it. Whether you want to be a business leader, teacher, plumber, motorcycle racer, mother, hair stylist,

143

salesperson, father, husband, wife, artist (or a combination of things), do it with your whole heart, mind, body and soul. Run a marathon, climb a mountain, see your grandchildren once a week, read a bestseller once a month, make a daily "to do" list and finish it, remember to daily tell your significant-other why you love him/her, make sure the dirty dishes go in the dishwasher before you go to bed–all of these are achievements, too.

Some achievements manifest money. **All** achievements manifest self-satisfaction, self-esteem, and self-worth.

Don't minimize what it is **YOU** want to accomplish, every achievement reached is a stepping stone to the next achievement. Often the smallest accomplishments bring about the greatest sense of achievement and catapult you into something much bigger.

Building Strong Personal Foundations

"To thine own self be true," Shakespeare said. Jesus said, "Love thy neighbor as thyself." These are tall orders. However, before you can even begin to be true to yourself or to love your neighbor, you have to know and love yourself.

I find it compelling how often the emphasis is put on "love your neighbor". The most difficult part is overlooked–"as thyself". Do you even know and like YOU? How do you show love to YOU? How do you talk to YOU? Do you know how to rest and retreat? Do you know what fun means for you and if so, do you do it?

Building strong personal foundations is about getting to know **YOU**. The foundational building blocks include: emotional, physical, spiritual and relational health and well being.

Emotional Health – How do you feel? Can you describe your feeling to someone else? I'm not talking about the typical, "I'm fine". I mean exactly "how do you feel?" Here is a list of feelings to explore, an emotional "gas gauge," if you will: joyful, happy, sad, pensive, melancholy, desperate, angry, ecstatic, triumphant, depressed, miserable, discouraged, determined encouraged, frustrated, anxious, worried, satisfied, uncomfortable, elated, vivacious, jubilant. There are hundreds of others.

Actions follow feelings and emotions. If you can figure out what you really feel at any given moment, you have the choice to shift or change it. To make a small shift in how you feel can result in huge changes in many aspects of life.

Our emotional make-up is developed the first three to five years of our lives. Like it or not, dealing with (working through, understanding or whatever you want to call it) your upbringing and family dynamics is a must for emotional health. My dad told me that once I became an adult I was responsible for my life. He told me to pick and choose what rang true for me internally from my upbringing and discard what didn't. He made it clear that I no longer had the luxury of pointing my finger at him or mom for what I felt was wrong with my life. Actions follow feelings and emotions.

Do Your Work!! Read and complete the exercises in books about family dynamics and self-esteem. Attend workshops and classes. Sign up for a weekend retreat. This is what I call the "work."

Good, old-fashioned therapy is an excellent option. I'm not talking about for 30 years once a week. I'm talking about working with a proven professional for a finite period of time on specific issues. I am eternally grateful to the mentors, coaches and therapists I've worked with over the past 30 years. Each opened new doors and helped me take my life to levels I never dreamed possible.

It takes great skill, perseverance, courage and love of self to embark on the journey into your emotional self-discovery. Facing your issues and working through them is an achievement that will truly catapult you to another level of life.

Physical Health – How well do you know your body? How do you treat it and what do you feed it? How do you keep it fit? Do you like being in your own skin and do you even know what that means? Would you rather be in someone else's skin? Where do you hold your tension? Where do you feel your joy, sadness, excitement, grief, pain?

Get body work done to relieve stress, such as massage, Rolfing, etc. Exercise: walk, run, yoga, cycle, dance. See your doctor regularly–eastern/western medicine, choose one or a combination of both. Whatever you do, do it consistently. Your body is the vehicle you use to manifest your achievements. Keep it in tip-top shape. This is not rocket science!

Spiritual Health – What do you believe? Have you ever wrestled with God, Creator, Higher-Power? Have you searched your heart, mind and soul for the meaning of life for YOU? Have you dissected what you were taught as a child regarding faith, religion and God? Do you own your beliefs? If you have a tradition–Buddhist, Muslin, Jew, Christian, do you practice it? Why or why not?

"We need a path. We are lost without one. Religions are homes. Religious community and tradition put us in touch with the wisdom and beauty of the past. They are communities of memory. There is much to be said for being part of a tradition centuries old rather than one made up yesterday."[1] Pick a path and start to walk!

Your spiritual belief systems impact your entire life and how you live it. It can be scary to really delve into this realm. This is the world of faith and on this path you look at your core beliefs about how the universe is run and your personal place within it.

If this is an area of your life you would like to focus on, you may want to consider working with a Spiritual Director. Spiritual Directors are "individuals who have been called to accompany others seeking the Mystery we name God."[2] They assist in the discovery of who God is for you and how you manifest God in your daily life.

Get clear about what you believe and make time for this relationship. It is an amazing, life-changing journey!

Relational Health – How are your personal relationships? In your obituary, will you be remembered as a cherished friend, wife, husband, sister, brother, mother, father? What does it mean to have a healthy relationship? How much time and effort are you willing to expend on relationships?

---

[1] The Heart of Christianity – Marcus J. Borg.
[2] Excerpt from the "Spiritual Directors International Mission Statement" – www.sdiworld.org

Developing and maintaining a healthy relationship is all about using communication and honesty and being your true self. These characteristics come from self knowledge and self awareness; they require quality time and effort. Because this aspect of my life is important to me, I have made manifesting healthy relationships with family, friends and business associates a goal and highly prized achievement.

The marriage or committed relationship is the most interesting. It is one of few opportunities in life where we get to observe ourselves in our true nature. When you live with someone you can't keep up pretenses forever. If you are blessed with children, then your true nature will arrive on the scene at unexpected times and places.

When your true nature does emerge, you are given a chance at a wonderful gift. You have the opportunity to take a long, hard look at yourself. If you want to know who you really are, ask your spouse or significant other. Ask your children. You will have to make sure to explain you want the honest, uncensored truth. You will have to promise not to get angry, interrupt, talk back, judge the response, yell or leave. And you have to promise not to hold it against them or throw it in their faces at a future date. This takes real guts.

And, the other side of that is asking your spouse or significant other to tell you who THEY really are, and what they REALLY feel, and what they REALLY want. Again, you must promise the same things I mention above. This takes unconditional love and a real desire to be intimate.

If you want to take it a step further, ask your friends and colleagues. It is an "eye-opening" process. After you collect the information, then it is decision time. Are you going to do the work or not?

Will you open this door of opportunity or run scared? The payoff? It's huge. Renewed passion--literally and figuratively. Freedom to be your true self with your spouse and family (the best place to start, and it will spill over into all your relationships over time). Inner peace. Voice--your own. Lightness of heart and spirit. Connection and intimacy on a level you may not know existed.

My husband and I have been together for 21 years; 19 of those years married. Yes, there were times when I wanted to give up. But, I'm a fighter and I was willing to "open the door" and seize the opportunity to really get to know my husband and myself. It took us about 17 years to "open our door" and now that we have, well it is truly a mystery and a wonder.

Opening the door to self and another is an achievement; it takes self awareness, effort, skill, perseverance and, most of all, courage. If you are one of the few willing to get to the raw, reality of your committed relationship, you will be one of the few to reap the benefits of breaking through to an amazing place in yourself and the other.

How did I get to this place? I did (and am still doing) my "work", I learned to set and maintain boundaries, I found my voice and I got honest with my spouse and myself. I was ready to take whatever consequences came from this very intimate place (and I do mean ANY consequences). It was difficult and scary and we still have work to do together, but to break out of our cocoon and enjoy the beauty of our wings is so worth all the effort.

149

While doing your self-discovery work, you will achieve a level of comfort in setting and maintaining personal boundaries. And, you will begin to find your voice. Your relationships will change, as the internal work begins to manifest externally.

It is interesting to me that most of us can maintain a career and some level of family life or "relational connectedness" without doing the "work", without setting and maintaining personal boundaries and without "finding our voice." But, is that all you want to maintain?

Whether you realize it or not, your belief systems around your emotional, physical, spiritual and relational health will impact your ability to achieve. Taking time to build your personal foundations is a key secret of achievement.

I wish I could give you a glimpse into the sparkle and joy you will experience. The deeper level of love and care you will be able to give others and yourself, and the sheer delight you will find in being in relationships once you bring your total self to the party!

Remember, this is a life long journey. As you mature on your path, stay awake, be aware and pay attention. You will know when something is awry. Stop and listen to your inner voice. Then, take time to take care of YOU.

Owning Your Journey

This is your life. Own it. If you want it to be different, you are the only one who can manifest the changes needed to make it different. About 30 years ago, I sat in my first "motivational speaker" program. The gentleman, whose name I can't recall, spoke for about an hour, and then he said, "You are exactly where you want to be or you would be somewhere else!" I often contemplate this statement. It brings me back to the realization that I must own my journey. But what does that mean?

Take responsibility for your choices. That's what it means, and this process begins with knowing yourself and doing your "work". Learn how to say "no" and mean it and drop the guilt around it. Learn how to say "yes" and then follow through with 100% plus effort, and complete the commitment.

Own how you feel and listen to your intuition. Ask how this situation makes me feel? Be brutally honest. Intuitively you know the answer. Don't kid yourself. Feel how you feel all the way--completely. Don't shove it under the rug just because you don't like it, or because it feels too good. Don't just try to ignore it. The feeling won't go away and it won't be ignored.

Sure, maybe you shelve your feelings for a period of time, but they will come back with a vengeance. Each situation or feeling brings an opportunity for self-awareness and knowledge. An opportunity to process "it" **now** - the feelings, the results of an action, your response to a situation - each an opportunity. An opportunity to shift "it". Own it. Take your power back! Then, just watch what happens when "it" comes 'round next time! You'll see it differently, process it more quickly and shift it faster!

Be gentle with yourself. Are there really any mistakes in life? It all depends on how you look at it. Every choice in life has consequences. When we are young, we often make choices without considering how it will affect us in the long run. Hopefully, we learn and grow from all our experiences. We begin to see 'choice' and the impact of it. Be kind to yourself. Every choice and the resulting consequences offer an opportunity to learn and grow if you have the courage to question and explore it.

Forgive yourself. Change your self talk. As you become more understanding and gentle with yourself, life will be brighter, and your encounters with others will be more rewarding and more fun. There will be peace in your heart.

Walk your talk. Build integrity into your life. Know your core values and beliefs and use them to live your life. Actions speak louder than words. Be the change you want to see in the world. It is exponential. That whole "one random act of kindness" thing sets your life at a "higher vibration"[3].

Lastly, find balance and harmony, in all things. You'll know it when you don't have it–find it. You'll know it when you do–strive to keep it!

No one on earth has your exact same personality, experiences and style. Whatever you choose to do in your life, no one can do it, say it, or be it quite like you. You are unique; one-of-a-kind. This is your life. Define it, build it, own it! Discover **your** secrets of achievement.

Blessings to you on your journey!

---

[3] The Highest Level of Enlightenment - David R. Hawkins, M.D., Ph.D.

Chapter 15

What if Socrates Was Your Coach?

Machen MacDonald

"The way to gain a good reputation is to endeavor to be what you desire to appear." Simple, concise, profound wisdom from the Greek philosopher, Socrates, who mentored and coached Plato who in turn went on to mentor and coach Aristotle. Imagine how this simple wisdom has perpetuated through the centuries and still impacts our thinking and behavior today. This is the real power of coaching. It is the intangible gift that keeps on giving.

"The desire to appear" is simply having a compelling vision of yourself and what you are building. In essence it is your ideal self-image. You either endeavor to carry out the actions of ultimately being that ideal or you do not. There is no in-

153

between. Helping people identify and crystallize their ideal self-image is an imperative deliverable for a coach. Evoking your team to then recognize the best and most empowering actions to take to form the habits that will manifest that ideal image is the coach's primary objective.

"We are what we repeatedly do. Excellence, then, is a habit."

Many people attempt to over-power their willpower to get things done not realizing that real accomplishment springs forth from the shadow of habits. Look at any successful person. They did not achieve success from occasional accomplishment but rather from the regular carrying out of simple actions known as habits. Note that these habits may not always be the pleasing kind. However, the achievers have developed the habit of doing the critical success factors necessary for achievement and thus propelling themselves to the status of the successful. All the while, the unsuccessful person is not willing to engage in these critical success factors but perhaps occasionally.

It has been said, our thoughts become our words, our words become our actions, our actions become our habits and our habits become our destiny. Therefore, we must endeavor on all those levels with varying intensity throughout all the different dynamics in which we engage. As a coach, part of our pivotal purpose is to help others prosper by perpetuating profitable habits. Typically, as coaches, we might think the goal is to impart our wisdom. We look forward to sharing with others what we know. The challenge is that there remains a balancing act of imparting our perceived wisdom to others while helping them to tap their own wisdom.

Socrates' brilliant deduction in recognizing "wisdom begins in wonder" can be viewed as the essence of great coaching. It is easy to impress people with what we already know. Our ego demands it of us. However, as a coach we must not be a hostage to our ego but rather a host to our wondrous wisdom. As coaches who affect others profoundly we must develop the skill of inquiry. Throughout this book you have been exposed to various styles of questioning and inquiry. As coaches, we must master the habit of provocative questioning. It often appears that so called experts are rewarded for their subject matter expertise and its application to expedite solutions. It is easily mistaken that it is their subject matter expertise and knowledge that is being rewarded. Upon closer inspection, it is the expert who does not fall prey to the obvious and familiar, thereby being inquisitive and postulating inquiry, who is the true master. In order to bring their questioning to a higher level they must, no doubt, build on varying perspectives that can only come with experience and study. Great accomplishments come from asking one more question from the place of not having the answer. Remember to not answer quickly; but rather seek to know how others derive their answer. For this will provide you the wisdom you seek.

Imagine what Socrates meant when he stated, "As for me, all I know is that I know nothing." As a manager and leader we must bring subject matter expertise to the table on a regular basis. We must have ability to impart that kind of wisdom in an articulate and understandable fashion so that our team is best equipped to move forward. Let's be real! That is perhaps a large factor of why you were promoted into management. As Socrates observed, "Employ your time in improving yourself by other men's writings, so that you shall gain easily what others have labored hard for." By practicing this modeling of other's successes you will have become successful indeed. Advise your

155

team to do the same. In addition, be aware that the managers who have long and successful tenure have developed the skill of not always sharing the answers but rather sharing through questions, the gift of allowing their team to come up with the answers themselves. In other words, they are good coaches in that they guide people to tap in to their own inner wisdom and challenge them to take action based on that wisdom.

Much of great coaching is simply helping people to gain the most empowering perspective of the situation at hand. It is imperative to realize that regardless of the circumstance people may find themselves in, they always have the power to choose the healthiest perspective from which to view that situation. This should always serve as a firm basis to propel good coaching. To help people realize it may not be as bad as it seems, remember and share these compelling words of Coach Socrates, "If all misfortunes were laid in one common heap whence everyone must take an equal portion, most people would be contented to take their own and depart."

A large part of successful coaching is helping people to become aware of and direct their emotions in the most empowering way. Consider that e-motion can be looked at as *energy* in *motion*. Find simple yet effective ways to help your people direct their energy in the proper motion that will enable them to achieve what they want.

One of the ways to do this is to help people realize that the quest is to happily achieve rather than trying to achieve in order to be happy. Let's face it, the ultimate goal as to why we engage in any endeavor is to be happy. We think making more money, buying the new sports car, getting married, going on vacation, or whatever it is, will make us feel happy and we therefore go after it. Then for many of us once we achieve that goal we feel happy for an instant and then start looking for something else to make us feel happy again. The inside insight to this is that the truly successful people are the ones that are feeling happy along the entire journey towards reaching their objectives; not just when they cross the finish line. They have found the strategy for being present and in the moment more often than not. While most everybody else is regretting the past and worried about the future, successful people are simply here in the moment and choosing to be happy. Yep! It's a choice. To help you make the best choice consider these words of Socrates, "Remember that there is nothing stable in human affairs; therefore avoid undue elation in prosperity, or undue depression in adversity." Coaching prowess is to help others become true to themselves and their purpose and ultimately follow their bliss and detach from the game of having their emotions anchored to the chaotic influences of others' opinions and agendas.

"The greatest way to live with honor in this world is to be what we pretend to be."

Pretend and intend to be a good coach. Endeavor to be a good coach, seek out good coaches and you are sure to become a good coach.

Since Socrates' time, the inspiring message of how to achieve success and fulfillment has traveled well. "Endeavor to be what you desire to appear." Over the past 24 centuries we have come to refer to it as, "fake it 'til you make it." I impart unto you: trust your inner wisdom, follow your heart and allow others to do the same and you will make it as a great coach. That's the power of coaching.

MEET OUR CARTOONISTS

Germaine Porche', MSOD and Jed Niederer CLU have successfully coached and consulted executives, teams and entrepreneurs in accelerating business performance internationally for more than 18 years. They have led workshops on leadership, breakthrough performance, communication, personal & organizational effectiveness, and coaching for more than 100,000 people in 15 countries.

Germaine and Jed co-authored *Coach Anyone About Anything: How to Help People Succeed in Business and Life*, which was listed among Amazon's Best 100 Business Books of 2003. Their new bestseller, *Coaching Soup for the Cartoon Soul*, points at the lighter side of Business & Life Coaching through their original cartoons, while highlighting useful coaching principles and concepts.

The American Business Women's Association named

Germaine one of the *Top Ten Businesswomen in America* for ABWA for 2006.

Jed earned degrees in Communications & Advertising from the University of Washington in Seattle, WA, and a Chartered Life Underwriter (CLU) degree from The American College in Bryn Mawr, PA. They can be reached at jed@eaglesview.com or gporche@eaglesview.com Telephone: 888-387-9786 or visit: www.eaglesview.com

The Business Coach will seldom give advice.

**However, when the
situation warrants
advice, the Coach will
give it based only
upon the most
rigorous of
business principles.**

The seasoned Coach has mastered the art of listening.

"The smallest of actions is always better than the noblest of intentions."

– Robin S. Sharma

"Man is what he believes."

- Anton Chekov

"Courage is not the absence of fear, but rather the judgment that something else is more important than fear."

– Ambrose Redmoon

Quick Order Form

The Power of Coaching
The Secrets of Achievement
By Machen MacDonald
$14.95

Shipping: $2.50 for first book
$1.25 for each additional book
(California residents add 8.25% sales tax)

Fax Orders	Telephone Orders
Send this form to: 530-687-8583	Call Toll Free: 1-530-273-8000 (Have your credit card ready)
Order On Line www.ThePowerOfCoaching.com	

Name _____

Address:_____

City/State/Zip:_____

Phone: _____

Email: _____

Method of Payment:

Visa   **Master Card**   **American Express**   **Discover**

Card Number:_____

Name on Card: _____

Expiration Date: _____

3-digit security code on back of card: _____

(If billing address is different from shipping address, please provide.)

167

NOTES